USING THE LEGEND

The amazing Superstars of WWE have earned no shortage of accolades. The table below lists the icons which illustrate the accolades featured on each Superstar's entry.

CHAMPIONSHIPS AND MORE!

ICON	DESCRIPTION
	Divas Search Winner
	Intercontinental Champion
	King of the Ring Winner
	Money in the Bank Winner
	Royal Rumble Match Winner
	Slammy Award Winner
	United States Champion
	Women's/Divas Champion*
	World Heavyweight Champion**
	World/WWE Tag Team Champion***
	WrestleMania Main Event Competitor
	WWE Hall of Famer
	WWE World Heavyweight Champion /WWE Champion****

* Recognizes WWE Women's Championship (1956–2010) and Divas Championship (2008–present)

** Recognizes NWA World Championship (pre-1991), WCW Championship (1991–2001) and World Heavyweight Championships won in WWE prior to unification with the WWE Championship (2002–2013)

*** Recognizes World Tag Team Championship (1971–2010) and WWE Tag Team Championship (2002–present)

**** Recognizes WWE Championship (1963–2013) and WWE World Heavyweight Championship (2013–present)

3

ADAM ROSE

The fun-loving Adam Rose always has a sweet taste in his mouth.

Adam Rose's party is just getting started. You can either be a lemon, or hop aboard the Exotic Express and be a rosebud. His colorful convoy (and for some reason, a giant rabbit) follows him wherever he goes. Rose's rowdy brigade even accompanies the flamboyant Superstar to the ring where Rose continues to let the good times roll. For a Superstar who ballyhoos around all day like he has just won the WWE Championship, it's hard to imagine the epic bash he'll throw if he ever does. The way he competes, that goal is not too far-fetched. Despite his festive personality, Rose is a dangerous competitor. His techniques are unorthodox yet effective. He is nearly impossible to prepare for. Just expect the unexpected from this free-spirited carouser, and enjoy the Rose Experience. Rose believes "it's party time all the time." So far, his entourage has plenty to celebrate.

An Adam Rose strawberry necklace makes a great party favor.

Adam Rose is ready to rock and roll all night in his leather vest.

HEIGHT: 6 feet, 1 inch (185 cm)

WEIGHT: 221 pounds (100 kg)

HOMETOWN:
Musha City, Bahamas

SIGNATURE MOVE:
Party Foul

MAKING AN ENTRANCE

Adam Rose made his debut by interrupting a rant by the surly Zeb Colter. Colter and Jack Swagger were hardly in a cheery mood, but Rose did not care. He led the Exotic Express in a conga line around the party poopers, kicking off a hostile rivalry.

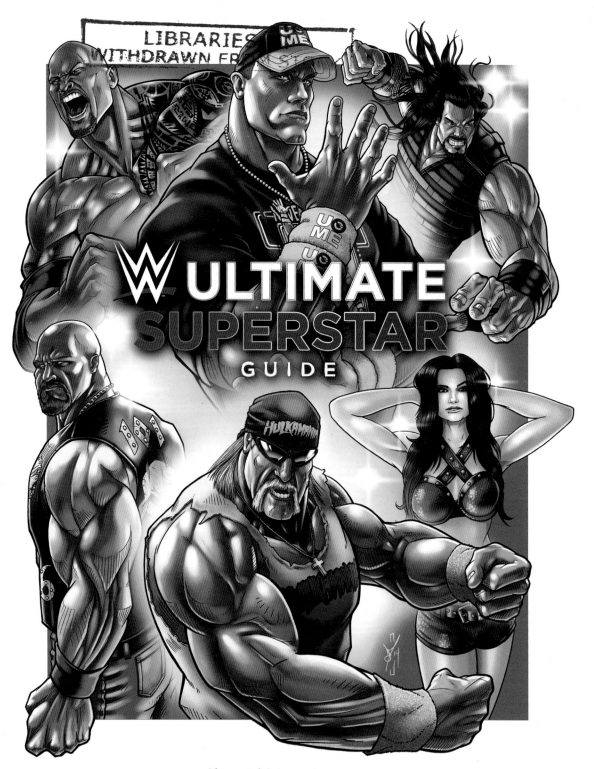

WWE ULTIMATE SUPERSTAR GUIDE

WRITTEN BY STEVE PANTALEO
ILLUSTRATED BY DAZ TIBBLES

DK | Penguin Random House

WELCOME TO THE WWE ULTIMATE SUPERSTAR GUIDE!

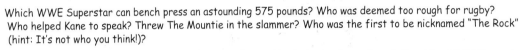

Which WWE Superstar can bench press an astounding 575 pounds? Who was deemed too rough for rugby? Who helped Kane to speak? Threw The Mountie in the slammer? Who was the first to be nicknamed "The Rock" (hint: It's not who you think!)?

It is these types of traits, quirks, abilities, attitudes, and little-known facts that distinguish a WWE Superstar from the pack. You will find them all here in the *WWE Ultimate Superstar Guide*. With over 200 new, vibrant illustrations blasting off each page, complete with lively bios and informative captions, the Superstars of Then, Now, and Forever have never been more captivating. No two, not even The Bellas, are completely alike. In fact, only one common thread links all Superstars from all generations—each has found some unique way of becoming larger-than-life. Now you can experience them like never before. Whether you need to sharpen your WWE acumen or are looking for the perfect companion for your next 24-hour WWE Network binge, you have come to the right place.

Over the years, you, the WWE Universe member, have played your own pivotal role in this book's creation. Your passionate cheers, jeers, signs, and chants have helped shape the continuing evolution of the Superstars currently sitting in the palm of your hand. We hope you enjoy your handiwork!

ADRIAN NEVILLE

Adrian Neville may not look like your prototypical WWE Superstar. The compact, humble kid from a mining town in northeast England may not boast about his incredible abilities either, but this promising NXT competitor has displayed technique beyond his years and amazing agility. He can also fly. His aerial exploits have earned him the nickname "The Man That Gravity Forgot." Since arriving in NXT he has racked up impressive accolades. He and fellow Brit Oliver Grey became the inaugural NXT Tag Team Champions by defeating the menacing Wyatt Family. At the groundbreaking WWE Network event, *NXT ArRIVAL*, Neville defeated a former ally, Bo Dallas, to become NXT Champion for the first time. As NXT Champion, he has successfully defended the gold against main roster Superstars such as Brodus Clay and Tyson Kidd. Gravity might have forgotten him, but Adrian Neville has all the tools to become a memorable WWE Superstar.

> Adrian Neville is proud to follow the footsteps of William Regal, British Bulldog, Bad News Barrett, and other British born Superstars.

> Neville is at his most impressive when he is leaping from the top turnbuckle. His Red Arrow finisher, a modified Shooting Star Press with a corkscrew twist of his body, is a sight to behold.

HEIGHT: 5 feet, 10 inches (178 cm)

WEIGHT: 194 pounds (88 kg)

HOMETOWN:
Newcastle upon Tyne, England

SIGNATURE MOVE: Red Arrow

NXT CAREER HIGHLIGHTS:
NXT Champion, NXT Tag Team Champion

SHOWSTOPPING PRAISE

Adrian Neville's NXT Championship victory over Bo Dallas was perhaps the biggest win in the burgeoning history of NXT. The main event of *NXT ArRIVAL* was the first Ladder Match in NXT history, and received a pre-match endorsement from none other than Ladder Match icon Shawn Michaels.

AFA

Afa's hair was as untamed as his feral persona.

Afa sported a mean looking Fu Manchu, which bristled whenever he growled.

Known simply in WWE as Afa, this WWE Hall of Famer carries the surname of the most fabled family in sports-entertainment: Anoa'i. After receiving training from family patriarch High Chief Peter Maivia, Afa formed a tag team with his brother Sika called The Wild Samoans. With the eccentric Captain Lou Albano steering their careers, the Samoans became one of the most feared and successful tag teams of all time. Their peculiar behavior and primitive habits terrified opponents, and that was before the bell rang. As competitors, they became even more untamed. Their vicious style won them three Tag Team Titles before they split. Afa returned to WWE in 1992 to manage the Headshrinkers, a team consisting of his son and nephew. His tutelage ensured that the Anoa'i legacy would continue. Now civilized, Afa and Sika can take credit for training countless future champions, including Yokozuna, Batista, Rikishi, and more.

The Wild Samoans would be considered one of the best teams to ever lace up a pair of boots, if they happened to own any.

HEIGHT: 6 feet, 2 inches (188 cm)

WEIGHT: 326 pounds (148 kg)

HOMETOWN: The Isle of Samoa

SIGNATURE MOVE:
Samoan Drop, Headbutt

FATHER AND SON

Once, while defending their Tag Team Championships from all comers, Sika was injured. Afa called in reinforcements in the form of his own son, Samu. Together, the father and son combo defended the titles until Sika returned.

AIDEN ENGLISH

Aiden English always accessorizes for the stage, showing off a variety of fine scarves and tiny hats.

Sports-entertainment is an art, one of many that Aiden English is looking to add to his virtuous portfolio. The "Master of Sophistication" fancies himself a genuine artiste, able to create a masterpiece in forums stretching from the stage, the screen, the opera, and everything in between. Paired with "The Gentleman Grappler" Simon Gotch, English has even crossed into classic, theatrical vaudeville. The Vaudevillians bring an old school flavor to NXT. Their black and white, piano-driven entrance sets the tone for a throwback performance worthy of the early 20th century. Do not get too caught up with his artsy persona, however. Aiden English is a physical competitor who is determined to prove that a drama king can be just as tough as any simple-minded brute. Act one of Aiden English's sports-entertainment career is just beginning. If he has it his way, WWE fans will be shouting for an encore.

HEIGHT: 6 feet, 3 inches (191 cm)

WEIGHT: 215 pounds (98 kg)

HOMETOWN: Chicago, IL

SIGNATURE MOVE:
Director's Cut, That's a Wrap

Aiden English has been known to blow an appreciative kiss to the crowd before and after unveiling one of his artful maneuvers.

POWERFUL PIPES

R-Truth may soon have company in the category of Superstars who sing their way to the ring. Aiden English began showing off his vocal skills while on a winning streak in 2013. This classically trained performer has the potential to win both the NXT Championship and *American Idol*.

AJ LEE

Choose your words carefully around AJ Lee. If you are misfortunate enough to push the wrong buttons in this devilish Diva's mind she is liable to go *cra*... well, you know. AJ has displayed a Pandora's Box of personalities since she first skipped her way down a WWE ramp, each as captivating as the next. Her whimsical ways have left the WWE Universe and a bevy of male Superstars perplexed, not to mention a bit smitten. Though a giant question mark always looms over her true motives, some facts are cut and dry. AJ can flat out dominate in the ring. She proved this by shattering the record for the longest Divas Championship reign in history. AJ loves flaunting this achievement while degrading her fellow Divas. She is beautiful, talented, and manipulative to the core. And she knows it. Word of advice—expect the unexpected from this geek-turned-black widow Diva.

Prior to being comfortable in her own punk rock inspired merchandise, AJ's head games involved wearing the shirts of ill-fated male suitors including CM Punk, Daniel Bryan, John Cena, Dolph Ziggler, and even Kane!

HEIGHT: 5 feet, 2 inches (157 cm)

HOMETOWN: Union City, NJ

SIGNATURE MOVE:
Black Widow, Shining Wizard

POSITIONS HELD:
Raw General Manager

I NOW PRONOUNCE YOU ... GENERAL MANAGER?

AJ shocked the world when she accepted an offer from Mr. McMahon to become *Raw* General Manager. Her tenure served as the official death knell for her twisted love saga with Daniel Bryan. Ironically, another controversial romance with John Cena led to her dismissal. AJ was memorable as GM but she has proven that the ring is where she belongs.

ALEX RILEY

A slap to the face from The Miz set Riley off in 2011. It was the last straw for "A-Ry." He fought back and struck out on his own to make an impact without his loudmouth mentor.

Alex Riley was an impressive competitor on season two of *WWE NXT*. He and his WWE Pro, The Miz, formed a bond that would last through The Awesome One's greatest run in WWE. Riley toted around Miz's Money in the Bank briefcase and later protected his interests as WWE Champion, all the while learning the ropes in WWE. He learned so well in fact that he actually scored a victory over his former mentor once their relationship turned sour. After some up and down success in the ring, Riley now puts his communications degree to use as a commentator. The lifelong jock and son of an ESPN sportscaster feels right at home behind an announcers' desk. "The Rare Breed" has been seen on pay-per-view panels, preshow events, and on *WWE NXT*. His mixture of in-ring experience and broadcasting pedigree shows in his analysis of all the WWE action.

Alex Riley debuted in WWE wearing a varsity letterman jacket but has since gone Banana Republic to clean up for commentary.

HEIGHT: 6 feet, 3 inches (191 cm)

WEIGHT: 236 pounds (107 kg)

HOMETOWN: Washington, D.C.

SIGNATURE MOVE:
Riley Elevation

MAIN EVENT MEDDLING
Alex Riley impacted the main event of *WrestleMania XXVII*. Still under the stewardship of The Miz, Riley accompanied the "Must-See" Champion to the ring to face John Cena. His interference helped spring Miz to a historic victory on the Grandest Stage.

ALEXA BLISS

The WWE Universe is about to discover their inner "Bliss-ness." Alexa Bliss is a pint-sized newcomer to WWE, currently getting noticed in the competitive NXT Divas division. This spunky Diva has a future as bright as her dazzling ring attire. She is quickly becoming NXT's sweetheart. Radiant from head to toe, Alexa wears a warm smile and a whole lot of glitter wherever she goes. No stranger to athletics, she has competed in softball, kickboxing, gymnastics, and Division 1 cheerleading. Now, the free-spirited fireplug has arrived in WWE. Despite her blissful demeanor, she knows WWE is no fairy tale and is prepared to do whatever it takes to succeed. She may be small in stature, but Alexa Bliss packs a concentrated dose of feistiness in her five-foot-one frame. If she maintains her positive outlook and work ethic, she will soon be brightening up the Divas competition on *Raw* and *SmackDown*.

Alexa Bliss has earned accolades in competitive bodybuilding. She credits the sport for giving her a much-needed boost in confidence.

HEIGHT: 5 feet, 1 inch (155 cm)

HOMETOWN: Columbus, OH

Alexa Bliss likes to be sparkly. She incorporates her signature shimmer into her tutu and ring gear in the hopes that it makes people smile.

AUSPICIOUS DEBUT

Bliss impressed in a tournament held to claim the title vacated by Paige shortly after *WrestleMania 30*. She scored an upset victory in round one against veteran Alicia Fox and lost to the eventual winner, Charlotte, in the semi-finals.

ALICIA FOX

Alicia has been known to add a foxy red shimmer to her coat.

Long black boots are a feature of most foxes in the wild.

Alicia Fox made history in 2010 by becoming the first ever African-American woman to win the Divas Championship. WWE had not seen a foxier champion before and hasn't since. Today, Alicia continues to mix it up in the Divas division with the same sly spunk that first caught the eye of the WWE Universe. Alicia's legs seem to stretch as far as the coastline of her home state of Florida. She uses these long limbs to her advantage, downing opponents with her signature Scissor Kick. "Foxy" is nimble, spirited, and tough within the ropes. Don't let her friendly face fool you. Foxes are versatile hunters and this vixen can adapt to any environment as she hunts for Divas' gold. And if you happen to be ringside for one of her bizarre, post-match tantrums, look out!

HEIGHT: 5 feet, 9 inches (175 cm)

HOMETOWN: Ponte Vedra Beach, FL

HOME WRECKER

Alicia Fox left an inauspicious first impression on the WWE Universe as the wedding planner for Edge and Vickie Guerrero. She shattered the first rule of wedding planning by locking lips with the groom to be. The treacherous act ruined any chance of a happy honeymoon, but not Alicia's career. After a sabbatical, she emerged reinvigorated and surprised everyone with her in-ring agility.

ANDRE THE GIANT

At 7'4", Andre towered over the most behemoth Superstars in WWE.

Andre the Giant is one of the most celebrated figures in WWE history. His gargantuan proportions and ring prowess captivated audiences and made him a worldwide attraction. For an incredible fifteen years, Andre remained undefeated, conquering several WWE legends along the way. At the first *WrestleMania*, he proved to be WWE's premier big man by winning Big John Studd's Bodyslam Challenge. Years later, he finally captured the WWE Championship, a richly deserved accolade. Andre's star crossed over into movies, where he played the gentle giant Fezzik in the hit comedy *The Princess Bride*, a fitting role for this beloved icon. One year after his passing, Andre was enshrined as the first inductee into the WWE Hall of Fame, a proper send-off for a man who was truly larger-than-life.

Andre's mono-strapped singlet is the archetype for a giant's ring gear.

Andre's massive boots are still on display at WWE Headquarters.

HEIGHT: 7 feet, 4 inches (224 cm)

WEIGHT: 520 pounds (236 kg)

HOMETOWN: Grenoble, France

SIGNATURE MOVE: Sitdown Splash, Double Underhook Suplex

NICKNAME: The Eighth Wonder of the World

THE SLAM HEARD 'ROUND THE WORLD

When Hulk Hogan slammed Andre at *WrestleMania III*, it signified the ultimate passing of the torch and a watershed moment in WWE history. At *WrestleMania 30*, Hogan initiated an Andre the Giant Memorial Battle Royal, ensuring that Andre's legacy continues in WWE.

ANGELO DAWKINS

Dawkins sports a custom made flat-brim with his initials, A.D.

Dawkins's glasses are more for fashion than for correcting his vision.

Dawkins listens to some fresh beats to get himself psyched for a match.

Angelo Dawkins is an impressive athlete looking to gain momentum on *WWE NXT*. No stranger to athletic achievements, Dawkins has made no bones about his desire to parlay his success into the world of sports-entertainment. The Cincinnati native has said he is "here to make a statement and to raise his game to the next level." A bold claim for a man who won national championships in three different college sports: wrestling, track, and football. The Bo Jackson of NXT, Angelo Dawkins is a multi-talented individual, even if he is blissfully unaware that dancing is not one of those talents. Dawkins is in his own zone all the time. He looks as if he stepped straight out of an old Run-DMC video and landed in NXT. Regardless of any fashion faux pas, this raw competitor is someone to watch out for in the near future.

HEIGHT: 6 feet, 5 inches (196 cm)
WEIGHT: 280 pounds (127 kg)
HOMETOWN: Cincinnati, OH

STICKING WITH IT

Dawkins incorporated hip-hop culture into his persona in April 2014. Since then, he has continued to show improvement. Dawkins is always upbeat and revels in the next challenge, no matter who is standing in his way.

BAD NEWS BARRETT

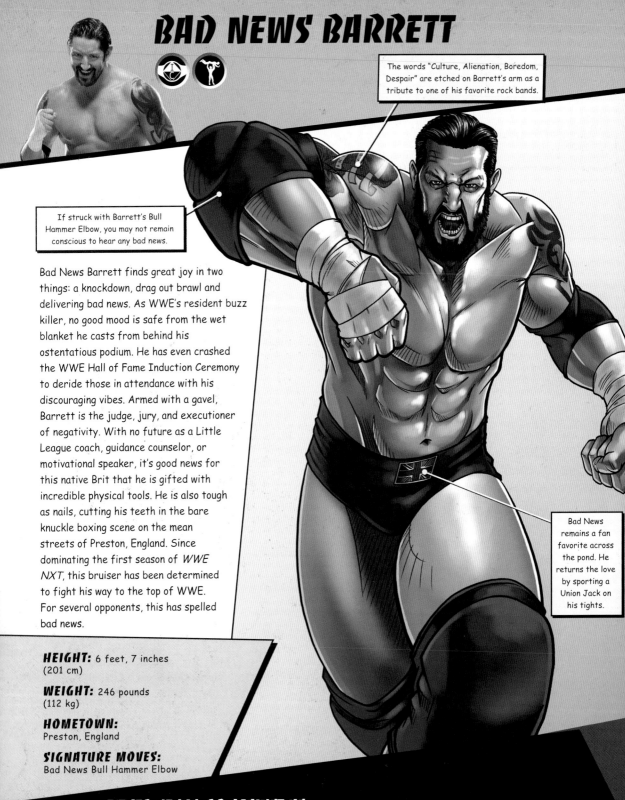

The words "Culture, Alienation, Boredom, Despair" are etched on Barrett's arm as a tribute to one of his favorite rock bands.

If struck with Barrett's Bull Hammer Elbow, you may not remain conscious to hear any bad news.

Bad News Barrett finds great joy in two things: a knockdown, drag out brawl and delivering bad news. As WWE's resident buzz killer, no good mood is safe from the wet blanket he casts from behind his ostentatious podium. He has even crashed the WWE Hall of Fame Induction Ceremony to deride those in attendance with his discouraging vibes. Armed with a gavel, Barrett is the judge, jury, and executioner of negativity. With no future as a Little League coach, guidance counselor, or motivational speaker, it's good news for this native Brit that he is gifted with incredible physical tools. He is also tough as nails, cutting his teeth in the bare knuckle boxing scene on the mean streets of Preston, England. Since dominating the first season of *WWE NXT*, this bruiser has been determined to fight his way to the top of WWE. For several opponents, this has spelled bad news.

Bad News remains a fan favorite across the pond. He returns the love by sporting a Union Jack on his tights.

HEIGHT: 6 feet, 7 inches
(201 cm)

WEIGHT: 246 pounds
(112 kg)

HOMETOWN:
Preston, England

SIGNATURE MOVES:
Bad News Bull Hammer Elbow

EITHER NEXUS, OR AGAINST US

Long before picking up a gavel, Bad News Barrett ruled the renegade faction The Nexus with an iron fist. Like a pack of wolves, Barrett and his black and yellow clad goons unleashed a ruthless streak of devastation

BAM BAM BIGELOW

Tattoos blanketed the back of Bigelow's head and came to a point in the front.

Known as the "Beast from the East," Bam Bam Bigelow left a sizable dent in WWE for much of the early to mid-1990s. The New Jersey native was born to be a sports-entertainment villain. His tapestry of head tattoos amplified his natural scowl. He had a scary look about him, and a surly demeanor to match. Bigelow clashed with everyone from Bret Hart to Doink the Clown, his athleticism catching many people off guard. No other big man in WWE history could pull off Bigelow's arsenal, which included a moonsault from the top rope, something unheard of for a man of his size. His mixture of brute strength and versatility led to some classic bouts. None were bigger than his lone *WrestleMania* main event. At *WrestleMania XI*, Bigelow stepped into the ring with football icon Lawrence Taylor. LT got the victory, but Bigelow's performance is still praised to this day.

Bigelow's unique ring attire covered his massive frame in black with flames dancing up each side.

HEIGHT: 6 feet, 4 inches (193 cm)

WEIGHT: 390 pounds (177 kg)

HOMETOWN: Asbury Park, NJ

SIGNATURE MOVE:
Greetings from Asbury Park

THE BATTLE FOR BAM BAM

While mostly known as a villain, Bam Bam began his WWE career as a good guy. He earned the fans' positive vibes by denouncing several crooked managers who were vying for his services. Bigelow teamed with Hulk Hogan at the first-ever *Survivor Series*, and even outlasted the Hulkster in the match.

BARON CORBIN

Baron Corbin has a colorful arrangement of tattoos covering his chest and crawling up and down his left arm.

Baron Corbin is a proven commodity in the rough-and-tumble cultures of both boxing and football. In his NFL career, he smashed defensive tackles as a member of both the Indianapolis Colts and Arizona Cardinals. Like most Superstars, Corbin desired to compete in WWE since he was a little kid. Having made the transition from the gridiron to NXT, he pursues his dream with "heavy hands and bad intentions." Corbin follows the footsteps of others such as Stone Cold, Goldberg, and JBL who also made the leap from pro football to sports-entertainment. A self-proclaimed "different breed," Corbin is also a three-time Golden Gloves boxing champion, giving him a dangerous skill set. With a chest full of tattoos and a mind filled with aggression, his presence is also intimidating. Corbin has been on a tear since *NXT Takeover: Fatal 4-Way*, racking up quick, decisive victories and seeming to grow hungrier after each three count.

HEIGHT: 6 feet, 8 inches (203 cm)
WEIGHT: 275 pounds (125 kg)
HOMETOWN: Kansas City, KS
SIGNATURE MOVE: End of Days

INSPIRED

Baron Corbin has experienced a packed University of Phoenix Stadium many times. For *WrestleMania XXVI*, he enjoyed it as a fan. In the stadium where he played his home games, Corbin witnessed the epic rematch between Undertaker and Shawn Michaels. It fueled his dream to compete in WWE.

BATISTA

Batista is covered with ink, adding to his intimidating look. His tattoos include the Greek and Philippine flags, a sun, a fire breathing dragon, and several others.

Batista once boasted, "Everything about me screams, 'Champion'." With six World Heavyweight Championships to his name, arguing is pointless. The Animal is an evolutionary force of nature. Raised on the coarse blacktops of Washington D.C., Batista honed his survival instincts at a young age. Tough-as-nails with the body of a Greek god, sports-entertainment was a natural fit. WCW trainers disagreed. WWE did not, and Batista has been an Animal possessed ever since. He does not care who is in front of him. He could care less what you think. Whether walking alone or with Evolution, when The Animal steps through the ropes, he believes he is stepping into his kingdom. There is only one thing on his mind, reclaiming his place at the top of the food chain.

HEIGHT: 6 feet, 6 inches (198 cm)

WEIGHT: 290 pounds (132 kg)

HOMETOWN: Washington D.C.

SIGNATURE MOVE: Batista Bomb

NICKNAME: The Animal

PAST, PRESENT & FUTURE

Triple H saw Batista's potential when he first arrived in WWE. The Game recruited the behemoth enforcer as well as Randy Orton to his Evolution stable. With Ric Flair acting as the sage from sports-entertainment's past, the group protected Triple H's World Heavyweight Title. Orton and Batista eventually broke out, winning several titles of their own. A decade later, Evolution reunited in an attempt to rid WWE of Daniel Bryan, The Shield, and others.

BAYLEY

A wide-eyed fan girl from California, Bayley is living a dream she has had since she was eleven years old. A lifelong athlete in sports such as basketball, track, and martial arts, Bayley's first love was sports-entertainment. It is only fitting that she makes her current home in Orlando, Florida, where she trains to be a future WWE Diva as part of WWE NXT. Rubbing elbows with Natalya and other veteran Divas she grew up idolizing, Bayley admits that she still gets butterflies from time to time. In the ring, she has teamed with Charlotte with some success. However, their friendship was short-lived. Charlotte attacked her during a match and joined the BFFs (Beautiful Fierce Females). Since then Bayley has teamed with Natalya and gotten her hands on Charlotte a few times, even challenging for the NXT Women's Championship. Bayley's hope is that an excited young girl watching today will some day idolize her.

HEIGHT: 5 feet, 6 inches (168 cm)

HOMETOWN: San Jose, CA

SIGNATURE MOVE:
Baley-to-Belly Suplex

SHWEET

NXT's most enthusiastic Diva once kept a video blog detailing her "shweet" experiences inside WWE's Performance Center. While she is quick to dole out hugs for everyone, she has proven capable up turning up her aggression inside the ring.

BECKY LYNCH

If Becky Lynch has her way, the future of the WWE Divas division will have a bit of an Irish flavor. Lynch shares a hometown with WWE Superstar Sheamus, and is already displaying the Dublin brand of tenacity fans have come to expect from her countrymen. The fiery redhead debuted on a June 2014 episode of *NXT*. She entertained fans by getting jiggy with it upon her entrance, but Lynch is not here to become Fandango's next dance partner. She handedly won her first match over Summer Rae, putting the rest of the NXT Divas on notice that she has come to fight. She made an impression on fellow NXT Diva Bayley, who quickly became an ally. Becky Lynch may be new to NXT, but she grew up inside a ring. She began training at age 15, dedicated her life to sports-entertainment and is ready to make an instant impact.

Becky Lynch's red hair, wild side, and daring moves in the ring remind some historians of WWE Hall of Fame Diva, Lita.

HEIGHT: 5 feet, 6 inches (168 cm)

HOMETOWN: Dublin, Ireland

The green in Becky Lynch's gear resembles the countryside of the Emerald Isle.

A NEW ATTITUDE

Since she first introduced herself to the NXT audience, Becky Lynch has shown she is more than just an Irish stereotype. She even rebooted her entrance routine to show the high-octane, aggressive rock and roll side of her personality.

BIG BOSS MAN

When Big Boss Man unleashed his handcuffs and signature nightstick, someone was about to sing the prison blues.

Big Boss Man's uniform commanded respect. Shoulder stars, a law enforcement shield, and three gold bars proclaimed his authoritative status.

Big Boss Man was a former prison guard who came to WWE determined to bring "hard times" on those who stepped out of line. Armed with a short nightstick and the long arm of the law, Big Boss Man's harsh brand of justice toed the boundaries of the American way throughout his long career. While aligned with the devious Slick, the towering cop abused his authority. His practice of cruel and unusual punishment led many to question the honor of his badge. Later in his career, the deeds he performed on the take from Mr. McMahon's corporation probably should have landed him behind bars himself. Nevertheless, Big Boss Man remains a nostalgic figure for his efforts to rid WWE of evildoers. He put The Mountie in the slammer and vanquished a dangerous ex-con known as Nailz. Without Big Boss Man, law and order has not been the same in WWE.

Big Boss Man wore a traditional blue officer's gear before switching to riot squad black in the late 1990s.

HEIGHT: 6 feet, 7 inches (201 cm)
WEIGHT: 330 pounds (150 kg)
HOMETOWN: Cobb County, GA

FUNERAL CRASHER

Big Boss Man committed some atrocities in his career, but none as appalling as his actions at the funeral of Big Show's father. The crooked enforcer dragged the casket away from the proceedings, enraging Big Show and anyone with a hint of morality.

BIG E

Big E puts up NFL lineman numbers on the bench press, maxing out at 575 pounds.

Looking for the weight room? Just follow Big E. Of course, after this walking Mack Truck loads up his barbell, there are no more steel plates left for anyone else to lift. Big E requires a crane to spot him on the bench press, and while his massive bulk is not a fit for certain doorways, it sure is for WWE. Knowing he has the strength to compete at any level, the youthful powerhouse has committed himself to honing his technical skills. Spending several months as the enforcer for the spry Dolph Ziggler aided his cause. The eclectic duo used their complementary gifts to earn a Tag Team Championship Match at *WrestleMania 29*. They fell short, but Big E's star was still rising. After separating from The Showoff, Big E muscled the Intercontinental Championship from Curtis Axel. Much like his biceps, Big E's potential is nearly immeasurable.

HEIGHT: 5 feet, 11 inches (180 cm)

WEIGHT: 290 pounds (132 kg)

HOMETOWN: Tampa, FL

SIGNATURE MOVES: Big Ending

Mark Henry has company in the strongman department. One of Big E's incredible feats of strength is his deadlift of over 800 pounds.

BIG I

The Intercontinental Championship is one of the most historic prizes in WWE. Big E lived up to his prestigious predecessors, defending the title for close to six months. During his reign, he toppled Damien Sandow, Jack Swagger, and even his former partner, Dolph Ziggler, before losing the title to Bad News Barrett at *Extreme Rules*.

BIG JOHN STUDD

Big John Studd wore a furry beard long before Daniel Bryan made it popular.

WWE is full of legendary giants, but few have cast their towering shadow across history as well as Big John Studd. After several successful stints in various territories, Studd solidified his Hall of Fame stature in WWE. During a golden age of sports-entertainment, Studd's collisions with Andre the Giant and Hulk Hogan were felt on the Richter scale across all forty-eight continental states. Many remember his defeat to Andre in the Bodyslam Challenge at the inaugural *WrestleMania*. However, it was Studd's forceful shaving that cost Andre his signature nest of hair months before the big event. The following year, he showed the NFL's big men that WWE was no joke, tossing "The Fridge" out of the ring. In 1989, he hurled several of his own peers over the ropes to win the second ever *Royal Rumble*. Today, Studd is celebrated as one of the true giants to step their massive feet in WWE.

People of average proportions could collapse under the weight of Studd's robe.

Big John Studd's legs looked like massive white pillars in his signature ring gear. Three vertical stars speckled his full-length tights.

HEIGHT: 6 feet, 10 inches (208 cm)

WEIGHT: 364 pounds (165 kg)

HOMETOWN:
Los Angeles, CA

SIGNATURE MOVE:
Reverse Bear Hug, Backbreaker

HEENAN FAMILY

Bobby Heenan instigated Big John Studd's rivalry with Andre the Giant when Studd was a member of the infamous Heenan Family. However, when Andre turned to Heenan's evil ways, the giant shoe was on the other foot. Studd rebelled against his former manager and stood up to the antagonistic Andre, earning the crowd's affection.

BIG SHOW

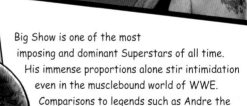

Big Show's chest measures an astounding 64 inches.

Big Show is one of the most imposing and dominant Superstars of all time. His immense proportions alone stir intimidation even in the musclebound world of WWE. Comparisons to legends such as Andre the Giant and Big John Studd are inevitable. However, Big Show distinguishes himself from his mammoth predecessors with a surprising agility that puts the "athlete" in World's Largest Athlete. He also possesses a sharp sense of humor. Make no mistake about it, though. Size matters. So does his mean streak. Big Show does not need any fancy catchphrases to get his point across. He just needs to stand up. Get in his way when he is angry and the result won't be pretty. He has left several top Superstars and even the ring itself in a heap of destruction. Cross this gentle giant at your own risk.

Big Show's cannonball of a fist is as devastating as any foreign object lurking under a WWE ring.

At size 22 EEEEEE, no one in the locker room takes home Big Show's boots by mistake.

HEIGHT: 7 feet (213 cm)

WEIGHT: 425 pounds (193 kg)

HOMETOWN: Tampa, FL

SIGNATURE MOVE: Chokeslam, KO Punch

SHOW BIG STRENGTH

Big Show debuted in WWE by hurling Stone Cold Steve Austin through a Steel Cage. Since then, his feats of strength have become legendary. He has overturned a two-ton Jeep, Chokeslammed JBL through the mat, and even tossed John Cena through a spotlight. Nothing is safe from his incredible power.

BILLY GUNN

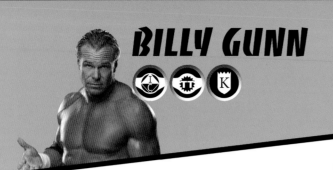

Billy Gunn might not be "new age" any longer, but outlaws last forever. From a heehaw cowboy caricature in the Smoking Gunns to "The One" and several incarnations in between, this gifted athlete has reinvented himself in seamless fashion over the years. His most famous—or rather, infamous—run came in the late '90s. Billy Gunn and Road Dogg embodied the cocky swagger of the Attitude Era, breaking it down with DX as the New Age Outlaws. The destructive duo ran roughshod over the tag team ranks, racking up titles at the expense of several legendary tandems and having a blast doing it. Long before social media existed, The Outlaws revolutionized crowd interaction, with fans belting out their signature lines. After a decade-long absence, the notorious rebels made a triumphant return to WWE, recapturing the Tag Team Titles. And if you're not down with that, Billy Gunn has some choice words for you.

Billy Gunn rocked a bandana during his days as an outlaw.

Billy Gunn adopted pink lips as a signature logo during the Attitude Era.

HEIGHT: 6 feet, 3 inches (191 cm)

WEIGHT: 260 pounds (118 kg)

HOMETOWN: Orlando, FL

HIRED GUNN

Though best known as a New Age Outlaw, Billy Gunn has proven to be a formidable ally to several tag team partners. His own brother Bart, his close pal Chuck Palumbo, Big Show, and Honky Tonk Man have all benefited from teaming with Gunn.

BO DALLAS

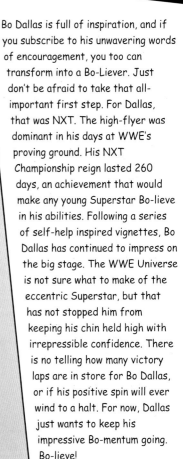

> Bo Dallas can see your true potential, and it brings a permanent smile to his face.

> Bo's ring attire is plain white, like the pages of your inspiring memoir that is just waiting to be written.

Bo Dallas is full of inspiration, and if you subscribe to his unwavering words of encouragement, you too can transform into a Bo-Liever. Just don't be afraid to take that all-important first step. For Dallas, that was NXT. The high-flyer was dominant in his days at WWE's proving ground. His NXT Championship reign lasted 260 days, an achievement that would make any young Superstar Bo-lieve in his abilities. Following a series of self-help inspired vignettes, Bo Dallas has continued to impress on the big stage. The WWE Universe is not sure what to make of the eccentric Superstar, but that has not stopped him from keeping his chin held high with irrepressible confidence. There is no telling how many victory laps are in store for Bo Dallas, or if his positive spin will ever wind to a halt. For now, Dallas just wants to keep his impressive Bo-mentum going. Bo-lieve!

HEIGHT: 6 feet, 1 inch (185 cm)

WEIGHT: 234 pounds (106 kg)

HOMETOWN:
Brooksville, FL

SIGNATURE MOVES:
Bo-Dog

HELPING HAND
Bo Dallas's reassuring words have no limits. Even during his pressure packed first months in WWE, he paused to lend some inspirational nuggets of wisdom to his fallen opponents. Few Superstars would pay such regard to someone who just tried to take their head off.

25

BOB BACKLUND

Backlund is the only man among the first 44 WWE Champions in history to have red hair.

Before Hulk Hogan defined Americana, before Stone Cold Steve Austin refused to submit, there was Bob Backlund. In the 1970s, Backlund's boy-next-door looks and refined technical skills brought the WWE Universe to a fever pitch. Backlund was a stark contrast to the flamboyant Superstar Billy Graham, whom he unseated as WWE Champion to the delight of a jam-packed Madison Square Garden. He would not relinquish the title for nearly six years, solidifying his place in WWE lore. Years after cultural changes drove him away from WWE, Backlund returned but still could not adapt to his New Generation contemporaries. He transformed into Mr. Backlund, a pontificating madman who used WWE as a pulpit to air his radical ideals. His condescending rants enraged fans, and vicious assaults using his Crossface Chickenwing added to the fury. This evolution from boyish hero to reviled lunatic makes him one of the most unique personalities ever enshrined in the WWE Hall of Fame.

Bob Backlund introduced this illustrious version of the WWE Championship. It features a giant, circular faceplate depicting a titlist with a globe behind him.

HEIGHT: 6 feet, 1 inch (185 cm)

WEIGHT: 234 pounds (106 kg)

HOMETOWN: Princeton, MN

SIGNATURE MOVE:
Crossface Chicken Wing

AN IRONIC TWIST OF FATE

When he lost the WWE Championship, Bob Backlund never succumbed to Iron Sheik's devastating Camel Clutch. His manager, Arnold Skaaland, threw in the towel. A decade later, he regained the title in the same fashion when Bret Hart's mother submitted to the maniacal Mr. Backlund on Hart's behalf.

BOBBY "THE BRAIN" HEENAN

Bobby Heenan was always scheming and concocting his next bit of mischief.

Bobby "The Brain" Heenan was an ingenious manager whose tutelage propelled a laundry list of talented competitors to stardom in WWE. Not a stable but a family, The Heenan Family lived by his bold mantra, "If you listen to me, you go straight to the top. If you don't, you're never heard from again." His clients listened, and so did the WWE Universe. Even though his underhanded tactics inspired chants of "weasel," his wit was undeniable. Heenan's way with words allowed him a seamless transition to the broadcast booth alongside the legendary Gorilla Monsoon. The verbal jousting from this tandem left viewers in stitches on a weekly basis. There was nothing in WWE that Bobby Heenan could not do, except wrestle that is. Regardless, who needs athletic ability when your nickname is The Brain?

Heenan dressed for ringside as if directing a masterpiece and in many ways, he was.

HOMETOWN:
Beverly Hills, CA

SUPERSTARS MANAGED: Andre the Giant, Mr. Perfect, Harley Race, Rick Rude, Big John Studd, The Blackjacks, King Kong Bundy, Nick Bockwinkel, The Brain Busters, Haku, Jesse Ventura, Ken Patera, Paul Orndorff, Hercules, and "The Narcissist" Lex Luger

THE IRRESISTIBLE FORCE
Andre the Giant's alliance with Bobby Heenan provided one of the tensest moments in WWE history. The Hulkster was beside himself at the sight. This betrayal set the stage for a monumental clash at *WrestleMania III*.

BOOKER T

Without his royal crown, Booker T's signature dreads whip furiously with each Spinaroonie.

Count 'em, Booker T was a five time (five time, five time, five time, five time!) WCW Champion.

Booker T is respected by today's WWE Universe for his strict but fair leadership as *SmackDown* General Manager. His decisive skills while overseeing the blue brand came as no surprise. As an in-ring competitor, he Spinaroonied his way to countless championships in both the tag team and singles ranks. Booker T boasted five WCW Championships before entering—or rather, invading—WWE in 2001 as the competition's ultimate titleist. Despite his WCW origins, the WWE Universe came to dig Booker T. He dazzled them with his potent offensive arsenal, highlighted by the spectacular, scissoring Axe Kick that showed his superior athleticism. His wildly entertaining partnership with the bizarre Goldust produced an unlikely chemistry. The duo won the Tag Team Championship and delivered countless unforgettable sound bites. In 2006, Booker T quite literally earned his crowning achievement in WWE when he won the King of the Ring tournament.

HEIGHT: 6 feet, 3 inches (191 cm)

WEIGHT: 253 pounds (115 kg)

HOMETOWN: Houston, TX

SIGNATURE MOVE:
Axe Kick, Spinaroonie

CATCHPHRASE:
"Can you dig it, sucka!"

ALL HAIL KING BOOKER
King Booker was the most majestic monarch in WWE history. Draped in a flowing red cape and armed with a golden scepter, he and his stately Queen Sharmell ruled *SmackDown* with an iron fist. His royal highness brought prestige to the throne by seizing the World Heavyweight Championship.

BRAD MADDOX

Maddox's plastic, politician's smile is easy to see through.

Many people would do anything for a job in WWE. A select few would infiltrate the referee roster and attack Ryback with a low blow from behind. Brad Maddox did just that. The desperate ploy earned Maddox the notoriety he craved and some retaliatory beatings. With WWE's attention, Maddox aspired to be an in-ring competitor. After it became clear he could not hack it, most thought he would fade away from the scene, a disgraced referee. Mr. McMahon thought differently. He gave the shameless brownnoser a job under Vickie Guerrero and soon after, Maddox was in charge of *Raw!* His reign as GM may have been short, but the era of "Bradtitude" brought plenty of controversy. Though fired by Stephanie McMahon, he is sure to resurface. No one knows what his next scheme will be, or to what depths he will sink to fulfill his delusions of grandeur.

If you saw Brad Maddox on the street in his vest and tie combo, you would think he was on his way to a college interview at Yale.

HEIGHT: 5 feet, 11 inches (180 cm)

WEIGHT: 207 pounds (94 kg)

HOMETOWN: Charlotte, NC

POSITIONS HELD:
Raw General Manager, Assistant to Vickie Guerrero

PINKSLIP FROM HELL
Sometimes wishing someone luck in their future endeavors is just not enough. The Authority wanted to put an exclamation point on Maddox's walking papers. So, they summoned Kane from the depths of Hell to deliver a Chokeslam and a Tombstone to

BRAY WYATT

Human nature is to fear what we do not understand. Menacing in his presence and mystifying to the masses, Bray Wyatt is the new face of fear. His presence brings an uneasy chill to the air. His sinister sermons and the actions that follow fracture the innocent psyche. Some may come to question their own existence, while others seek "false idols" to come to their rescue. Others, like Erick Rowan and Luke Harper, just follow the buzzards. Wyatt's menacing goons are spellbound by his every word, forming a sycophantic force field around the self-professed Eater of Worlds. Wyatt spreads his chilling message through cryptic, eerie prose as his freakish enforcers assist with his dirty deeds inside the ring. Whether surveying the carnage from a creaky rocking chair, creeping people out with his spider-walk, or unleashing Sister Abigail, everything Wyatt does serves some higher purpose. What purpose that is ... we probably don't want to know.

Wyatt keeps a tangled growth of facial hair and his loyal disciples do the same.

The Wyatt Family's lantern casts an ominous glow into the darkness.

Only Bray Wyatt can make such a festive wardrobe look terrifying.

HEIGHT: 6 feet, 3 inches (191 cm)

WEIGHT: 285 pounds (129 kg)

SIGNATURE MOVE: Sister Abigail

THE WHOLE WORLD IN HIS HANDS?

For months, the demonic Wyatt played mind games with John Cena, attempting to unleash the monster he insisted lurked inside of him. Cena stayed true to his code of hustle, loyalty and respect, but the Eater of Worlds converted some of Cenation's younger members in the process.

BRET "HIT MAN" HART

In the world of WWE, proclaiming one's self as "the best" is a way of life, but few Superstars have backed up this claim quite like Bret Hart. The son of Canada's wrestling patriarch, Stu Hart, Bret learned his craft in the illustrious Hart family dungeon. As a WWE Superstar, Bret spent well over a decade as the preeminent mat-technician in sports-entertainment. Clad in pink and black, the Hit Man plied his skills against a never-ending gauntlet of Superstars. From the mammoth Yokozuna to the wily Roddy Piper, Bret's mastery between the ropes had no bounds. He took on all comers, showcasing his unlimited arsenal of moves and counter-moves. Fans took notice, and Bret became an idol for a generation of WWE fans. Today, his career reads like a manual for anyone with aspirations of becoming a WWE Champion.

Bret Hart always gifted his trademark sunglasses to a deserving young fan sitting ringside.

Bret's pink and black getup is as synonymous with Canada as the maple leaf.

HEIGHT: 6 feet (183 cm)

WEIGHT: 235 pounds (107 kg)

HOMETOWN: Calgary, Alberta

SIGNATURE MOVE:
Sharpshooter

NICKNAME:
The Excellence
of Execution

DYNASTY

From the iconic Hart Foundation to contemporaries like Natalya and Tyson Kidd, the Hart family tree comprises a prestigious lineage of top notch WWE Superstars.

BRIAN KNOBBS

Knobbs merged the Mohawk and the mullet into one "nasticized" hair style.

During a colorful age in WWE, Knobbs stood out in his chain-linked black trench coat.

The Nasty Boys looked bad to the bone in their wraparound shades.

No one is certain where Nastyville is located within The Nasty Boys' native home of Allentown, PA. We can only assume it is on the wrong side of the tracks. Brian Knobbs looked and acted like every mother's worst nightmare. He was rude, rough, and just plain nasty. He and his partner Jerry Sags battered opponents in several stops throughout sports-entertainment. They came and went like a pair of rowdy bar-hoppers, leaving a trail of wreckage behind them. The burly street thugs were a scourge in WWE for three years. They shared the tag team turf with other smash mouth hoods such as The Road Warriors, Bushwhackers, and Demolition. They even took their graffiti decked outfits into *WrestleMania VII* and grabbed the World Tag Team Championships from the Hart Foundation. Knobbs was rarely seen without his toothless other half, Sags. Mess with one, the other is right around the corner.

HEIGHT: 6 feet, 4 inches (193 cm)

WEIGHT: 306 pounds (139 kg)

HOMETOWN: Nastyville

SIGNATURE MOVE:
Pit Stop, Trip to Nastyville

STENCH OF THE SOUTH

The Nasty Boys' manager, Jimmy Hart, did not know who he was trifling with when he betrayed the team in favor of Money, Inc. Knobbs called him a "little runt," earning cheers from the crowd. Then he introduced him to his sweaty armpit and unleashed a beat down.

BRIAN PILLMAN

Prior to his WWE career, Pillman was part of a tag team called The Hollywood Blondes. Little did he know his partner, Steve Austin, would end up his most bitter rival years later.

After unleashing his wild side, Pillman began wearing a black vest and grittier, more rebellious attire.

Brian Pillman was a gifted athlete who could be counted on to deliver a thrilling, spirited performance from bell to bell. Everything else was impossible to predict. Pillman began his career as a smiling, all-American high flyer, but most fans remember the "Loose Cannon," a crazy eyed lunatic with zero inhibitions. Pillman acted on impulse, with no filter to his words or actions. He seemed to harbor a deep-seated madness that worked its way to the surface as his career progressed. His outspoken venom got him fired from WCW. WWE had similar success fanning the flames of his hotheaded persona. Anything could set him off at any time. Though he was injured, The New Hart Foundation saw a potential ally in the volatile Superstar. Stone Cold was not as thrilled with Pillman's presence in WWE. Pillman's rivalries with The Rattlesnake and Goldust were intense and controversial, a precursor to The Attitude Era.

Brian Pillman's ankle injury prevented him from reaching his full potential in a WWE ring.

HEIGHT: 6 feet (183 cm)

WEIGHT: 227 pounds (103 kg)

HOMETOWN: Cincinnati, OH

SIGNATURE MOVE: Air Pillman

BIZARRE LOVE TRIANGLE

Brian Pillman had no limits, including Goldust's wife Marlena. Pillman wreaked havoc on The Bizarre One's marriage. He aired a series of disturbing videos making unflattering claims about his involvement with the gold clad vixen.

BRIE BELLA

The Bellas left fans broken-hearted in 2012 by stepping away from sports-entertainment. Thankfully, they returned in 2013 to dazzle the WWE Universe once again.

Brie Bella and Stephanie McMahon had each other arrested to gain leverage during their intense 2014 rivalry. Though Brie left *Raw* in cuffs, she was out of the clink in time to get her hands on the boss at *SummerSlam*.

HEIGHT:
5 feet, 6 inches (168 cm)

HOMETOWN:
Scottsdale, AZ

You're not seeing double. That is Brie Bella, the magnificent mirror image of her sister, Nikki. Together, the twin Total Divas are out to prove that two is always better than one. Whether stirring controversy in the Divas division or hoodwinking hapless referees with their mischievous "Twin Magic" maneuver, The Bellas always command the attention of the WWE Universe. The sisters possess a deadly combination of beauty, brains and determination. These compelling qualities have allowed them to parlay their success from the ring to reality TV. While the viewing public is delighted with this popular peek behind the curtain, it has drawn the ire of AJ Lee and other jilted Divas. The dissension within the ranks has only fueled Brie, who has fought for years to prove that she is not just camera fodder. The Bellas may be pretty, but what happens to you will not be if you underestimate these two former Divas Champions.

SHE SAID "YES!"

On an episode of *Total Divas*, Brie Bella agreed to tie the knot with her longtime boyfriend, Daniel Bryan. The "Yes!" Man and Brie were married just days after Bryan's monumental victory at *WrestleMania 30*. Though it has made her a target for hellish antagonists such as Kane, Bryan protects his better half like a bearded Superman.

BRITISH BULLDOG

Davey Boy's amazing feats of strength included hoisting a competitor from the ground to his shoulders with one arm.

Davey Boy Smith, aka British Bulldog, came to WWE from across the pond in merry old England, but if you are thinking of some tea-sipping stereotype, think again. The Bulldog possessed incredible strength and is a survivor of the infamous Hart Family Dungeon. It was there that he met his future wife, a sister of Bret and Owen Hart. Davey Boy fit right into the Hart family legacy, fighting both alongside and against his in-laws. The rivalry between the British Bulldogs and Hart Foundation set a new standard for tag team competition, their breathtaking matches oftentimes stealing the show. Davey Boy would join up with the New Hart Foundation later on, but not before proving his mettle as a standalone star. His definitive moment came in front of 80,000 countrymen in London's Wembley Stadium. The partisan crowd witnessed Bulldog defeat Bret Hart in a masterpiece for the Intercontinental Title.

HEIGHT: 5 feet, 11 inches (180 cm)

WEIGHT: 260 pounds (118 kg)

HOMETOWN: Manchester, England

SIGNATURE MOVE: Running Powerslam

Bulldog's loyalty to the queen was always on full display with a Union Jack splayed across his ring attire.

FITTING HONOR

Who better than a British Superstar to be the first ever European Champion in WWE? That is exactly what British Bulldog accomplished in 1997, winning a tournament hosted in Germany. The Bulldog topped his own Tag Team Championship partner, Owen Hart, in the finals.

BROCK LESNAR

Brock Lesnar cares about one thing, the pain he inflicts. He hails from Minnesota, but that is where his similarities with other humans end. Lesnar is a genetic anomaly, engineered for destruction and powered by hostility for everything standing in his path. He locks onto his target with the sick tunnel vision of a beast possessed and destroys it with the merciless force of an F-5 tornado. He derives no joy from "entertainment." Only twisted, beaten wreckage brings a satisfied grin to his face, whether in WWE or in other arenas he has conquered. At *WrestleMania 30*, he accomplished the unthinkable, breaking Undertaker's vaunted 21-0 undefeated Streak. He and his sleazy advocate, Paul Heyman, reveled in shaking the WWE Universe to its core, crushing their dreams of seeing their hero ride off into the sunset unblemished. With a Beast Incarnate lurking, nothing in WWE will ever be taken for granted again.

A tattoo of a sword framed by Brock's massive chest adds to his intimidation factor.

Lesnar's brutal offensive assault stems from his MMA experience, as do his black, fingerless gloves.

Brock Lesnar wears a threatening black and red color combo on his trunks.

HEIGHT: 6 feet, 3 inches (191 cm)

WEIGHT: 286 pounds (130 kg)

HOMETOWN: Minneapolis, MN

SIGNATURE MOVES: F-5, Kimura Lock

THE NEXT BIG THING

Paul Heyman may not always tell the truth, but he was not lying when he touted Lesnar as "the next big thing" in 2002. The dominant former amateur soon became the youngest WWE Champion in history. Since then he has brought a new level of carnage to WWE.

BROOKLYN BRAWLER

Brooklyn Brawler always looked as though he had just been through an alley fight. His stained, tattered wardrobe was as pretty as his unfortunate win-loss record. When he first emerged from the curtain, you weren't sure whether he was there to compete or to beg for subway tokens, but Brawler was no bum. He learned how to scrap in the rough, concrete jungles of his hometown New York City. Although he ended his matches staring up at the rafters more often than not, he never backed down from the biggest Superstars of the '80s and '90s. The gruff, hardnosed competitor has been a sentimental favorite in WWE for over two decades. Though his active career is over, he is always ready for a brawl. He made a surprise return in his home borough for the *TLC 2012* event. In a tag match, Brawler scored the winning submission wearing Brooklyn Nets garb.

Brooklyn Brawler's t-shirt never appeared washed and was always disheveled.

Brooklyn Brawler was usually seen with a stubby, unlit cigar dangling from his mouth.

HEIGHT: 6 feet (183 cm)

WEIGHT: 248 pounds (113 kg)

HOMETOWN:
Brooklyn, NY

SIGNATURE MOVE:
Sidewalk Smash

FRONT RUNNER?

After the New York Yankees' stunning defeat to the Boston Red Sox in the 2004 playoffs, Brooklyn Brawler renounced his home town. He changed his name to the Boston Brawler. This did not sit well with the Big Apple faithful, but Brawler has since taken back this Beantown indiscretion.

BRUNO SAMMARTINO

Bruno Sammartino held the WWE Championship for nearly eight years, by far the longest reign in history and a feat that will never be duplicated. An Italian immigrant, Bruno embodied the hopes and dreams of WWE's hometown fan base in diverse New York City. People from all walks of life rallied behind this distinguished strongman, flocking to Madison Square Garden in droves. Sammartino sold out The World's Most Famous Arena a mind-blowing 187 times. Like a living superhero, he defended the ultimate prize against a cavalcade of infamous villains. When his legendary run ended, fans were beside themselves in shock, a scene that resembled Undertaker's loss at *WrestleMania 30*. Bruno regained the title two years later and, true to form, held it for another three and a half years. This beloved legend received his long overdue induction into the WWE Hall of Fame in 2013. It was poetic happenstance that the emotional ceremony was held in the house that Bruno built, Madison Square Garden.

Bruno's barrel chest and record 565-pound bench press were a testament to his world-class strength.

Bruno was the second and final Champion to wear the Original WWE Championship, crafted on brick-colored leather with a gold faceplate of the United States.

HEIGHT: 5 feet, 10 inches (178 cm)

WEIGHT: 265 pounds (120 kg)

HOMETOWN:
Abruzzi, Italy; Pittsburgh, PA

SIGNATURE MOVES:
Bear Hug, Backbreaker

SHOWDOWN AT SHEA
Bruno Sammartino's drawing power extended from the arena to the massive Shea Stadium. More than 35,000 fans turned out to see Bruno clash with former protégé Larry Zbyszko in a Steel Cage main event. A preliminary match that

BULL DEMPSEY

Raised by the mean streets of Brooklyn, Bull Dempsey had no choice but to grow up tough. Dempsey had to learn how to fight at a very young age. Not only did he learn, he came to live for it. While other kids studied algebra, Dempsey studied history's most feared brawlers. He first stepped through the ropes at seventeen years old. Today, he plans to use his knowledge and natural physical presence to decimate his rivals in NXT. He considers himself "The Last of a Dying Breed." Dempsey's style is as pretty as a wrecking ball. He is just an old school brawler who loves a good fight. Every movement is made with full force. His rib-rattling body slam, which he has dubbed the Bulldozer, shakes the foundation of Full Sail University. It won't be long before his theme song inspires chants of "Bull! Bull Bull!" from the WWE Universe.

Chains draped over his neck let everyone know that Dempsey is bad to the bone.

Bull Dempsey's singlet is reminiscent of King Kong Bundy, a classic brawler who once clashed with Hulk Hogan.

HEIGHT: 6 feet, 2 inches (188 cm)

WEIGHT: 300 pounds (136 kg)

HOMETOWN: Brooklyn, NY

SIGNATURE MOVE: Bulldozer

NO BULL

Bull Dempsey made a successful NXT debut in June 2014. His victory put the rest of the locker room on notice immediately when the throwback mauler defeated Xavier Woods, a more experienced competitor.

BUSHWHACKER BUTCH

The Bushwhackers were two of the wackiest Superstars ever to lace up a pair of boots (which in their case were combat boots). Difficult to understand and even harder to tell apart, the fun-loving duo came stomping into WWE in 1988, endlessly swinging their tattooed arms with excitement. Butch and his cousin Luke originated from the vast outback of New Zealand. They never brought the Tag Team Championships back to their rugged home, but their shenanigans endeared them to the WWE Universe. Butch and Luke returned the affection by licking the heads of their admirers on the way to the ring. Rival teams were not so amused, and the cousins were hated by most of their peers. The hostility did not wipe the toothless smiles off their faces, though. Wins were few and far between, but win or lose The Bushwhackers carried themselves with oblivious joy, just living for the moment.

Despite the camouflage, Butch was extremely visible for several years in WWE. He and Luke clashed with many top tag teams of the '80s and '90s.

HEIGHT: 6 feet, 1 inch (185 cm)

WEIGHT: 249 pounds (113 kg)

HOMETOWN:
Auckland, New Zealand

SIGNATURE MOVES:
Double Gut Buster, Battering Ram

NO JOKE

It is misguided to knock The Bushwhackers less-than-stellar ring record. The wild ruffians have some impressive feathers in their bald caps. Their triumph over the Rougeaus gave them a victory at *WrestleMania*, something a select few can claim. Butch himself also scored an elimination in the most appropriate of places—the Gimmick Battle Royal at

BUSHWHACKER LUKE

Licking the heads of random spectators could not have been good for Luke's oral hygiene.

To go with their camo pants, The Bushwhackers wore uniform tank tops.

The Bushwhackers came to WWE by way of New Zealand, though they behaved as if from another planet. Mean Gene Okerlund gave audiences the exclusive look at their original habitat in the early '90s. The barbaric living arrangements and sardine-packed meals explained their crude habits in the ring. Luke and Butch were cousins, but could have been body doubles. Both were devoid of hair and teeth, yet full of cheery excitement. When they tugged on their signature camouflage pants and combat boots, there was no deciphering the roughhousing duo. Luke did set one unfortunate record all by himself at the 1991 *Royal Rumble*. Four seconds after entering the fray, he was dumped over the top rope. This did not repress his jovial outlook, as he strode back to the curtain with the same enthusiastic arm-swinging fans had grown to love. The Bushwhackers were non-stop fun, and are still imitated today.

HEIGHT: 6 feet (183 cm)

WEIGHT: 247 pounds (112 kg)

HOMETOWN: Auckland, New Zealand

SIGNATURE MOVE: Double Gut Buster, Battering Ram

CLOWNING AROUND

Luke and Butch found a like-minded Superstar in Doink the Clown. The Bushwhackers assisted the notorious prankster when he targeted the gruff Bam Bam Bigelow. The oddballs could not tickle Bam Bam's funny bone but did

BYRON SAXTON

Byron Saxton is a multi-talented individual who has made the leap from in-ring competition to announcing. As comfortable in front of the camera as a fish in the water, Saxton has been seen mostly as an announcer for NXT. He has also recently provided commentary on *WWE Main Event* and has conducted several interviews for the WWE App. Prior to becoming a full time broadcaster, Saxton spent two seasons as a NXT Rookie. Despite his solid physique and fearless style in the ring, he was eliminated both seasons. All was not lost, however. Saxton's infectious smile is undeniable, and WWE saw enough charisma to give him a chance behind a microphone. So far, Saxton has not disappointed. He has the benefit of having spent time in the ring learning from some of the best ring technicians in WWE. This experience plus his engaging personality are a great formula for success.

Though he no longer competes, Saxton is still not out of the line of fire. Alicia Fox got in his face at ringside during one of her bizarre meltdowns on *Main Event*.

In addition to his charming broadcasting voice, Saxton can also sing. He once survived another week in NXT by winning a karaoke contest.

HEIGHT:
6 feet, 1 inch
(185 cm)

WEIGHT: 212 pounds (96 kg)

HOMETOWN: Burke, VA

BIG LEAGUE

On the *NXT Redemption* season, Saxton showed a more fierce side to his personality. When things were not going his way, he "emancipated" himself from his Pro, Yoshi Tatsu, attacking him and referring to himself as "Big League" Byron Saxton. The strategy backfired, however. Saxton was eliminated soon after.

CAMERON

Cameron is not just an encyclopedia of dance moves. She has hit the books enough to earn degrees in marketing and psychology.

Cameron grooved her way into the hearts of the WWE Universe as one half of the Funkadactyls. With her former Diva dance partner Naomi, she rang in the arrival of Brodus Clay to the ring. But when the fun loving Funkasaurus became extinct, the two Divas decided to take a different orbit around Planet Funk. On her own, Cameron nearly struck gold at *Elimination Chamber 2014*. She defeated reigning Diva's Champion AJ Lee, but AJ's disqualification prevented the title from changing hands. Nevertheless, Cameron proved she has more than just rhythm. Fans of *Total Divas* will tell you—this radiant beauty has the brains, talent, and spunk to go a long way in WWE. Since the Funkadactyls split, she has looked more determined than ever. As Diva's competition continues to heat up, Cameron will be right there in the mix, looking to extend her dance floor dominance to the canvas.

Cameron's glittery gear comes in several colors, all equally dazzling to the eye.

HOMETOWN: Northridge, CA

HEIGHT: 5 feet, 4 inches (163 cm)

TOUGH ENOUGH

Cameron was one of the contestants on the popular revival of *Tough Enough* in 2011. After being the first contestant eliminated, it would have been easy for Cameron to throw in the towel on a sports-entertainment career. One year later, however, she was dancing under the bright lights of WWE, proving she was indeed tough enough.

CESARO

Cesaro is a fine-tuned athletic specimen with a universal spectrum of cultural knowledge. His ability to speak five different languages is a powerful skill for the jet setting life of a WWE Superstar. No matter where the plane lands, the "King of Swing" feels like he has the home field advantage. In his real home, Switzerland, he sculpted his body into such a lethal weapon he was deemed too rough for rugby. The Swiss Superman descended on the United States and true to form, he fit in like a chameleon. Cesaro dominated as the United States Champion and even impressed the nationalistic radical Zeb Colter. His career defining victory came in the Andre the Giant Memorial Battle Royal at *WrestleMania 30* when he slammed the massive Big Show over the ropes to claim the trophy. The next day he revealed himself as a "Paul Heyman Guy," becoming even more dangerous.

Simple wrestling shorts are embroidered with a "C" for Cesaro.

HEIGHT: 6 feet, 5 inches (196 cm)

WEIGHT: 232 pounds (105 kg)

HOMETOWN: Lucerne, Switzerland

SIGNATURE MOVES: The Neutralizer, The King of Swing

Cesaro's unique thigh wraps, instead of the customary knee pads, give him an authentic, throwback look.

KING OF SWING

The Cesaro Swing requires superhuman strength from every muscle in the body. Hooking the legs at waist height, Cesaro elevates his opponents off the ground and slings them around in a dizzying circle. The crowd pleasing move shows why Cesaro might be pound-for-pound WWE's strongest competitor.

CHARLOTTE

She may not wear flowing, sequined robes, but Charlotte still styles and profiles in her own way.

There are second-generation competitors, and there are those who were raised by a 16-time World Champion. Charlotte is the latter. Perhaps this is why in a short time, the daughter of Ric Flair is already a championship caliber player among the NXT Divas. Her father had a saying, "Diamonds are forever, and so is Ric Flair." This catch phrase is now evolving into a prophecy as the next generation of Flairs carries on the legacy. Charlotte is not averse to taking a page from her father's dirty playbook. As part of the BFFs (Beautiful Fierce Females), she showed, well, a flair for rule breaking. Since then, however, she has evolved into a fan favorite as the NXT faithful cannot help but cheer her athletic ability. Charlotte is not resting on the laurels of being a Hall of Famer's daughter. She is paving her own path and, so far, it is a successful one.

HEIGHT:
5 feet, 10 inches (178 cm)

HOMETOWN: The Queen City

SIGNATURE MOVES: Natural Selection, Figure-Four Leg Lock

NXT CAREER HIGHLIGHT:
NXT Women's Champion

FIRST OF MANY?

After only two years in NXT, Charlotte won a tournament to become the NXT Women's Champion. She defeated another second-generation Diva and a former WWE Divas Champion, Natalya, in the finals. Such an impressive win this early in her career should make all the WWE Divas leery of when this vicious competitor gets the call to the big time.

CHRIS JERICHO

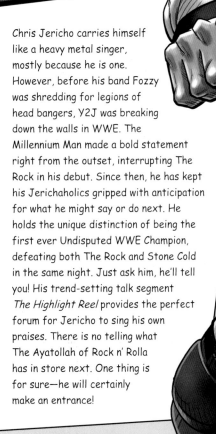

Chris Jericho's hairstyle has varied over the years but is always fit for the stage.

Chris Jericho carries himself like a heavy metal singer, mostly because he is one. However, before his band Fozzy was shredding for legions of head bangers, Y2J was breaking down the walls in WWE. The Millennium Man made a bold statement right from the outset, interrupting The Rock in his debut. Since then, he has kept his Jerichaholics gripped with anticipation for what he might say or do next. He holds the unique distinction of being the first ever Undisputed WWE Champion, defeating both The Rock and Stone Cold in the same night. Just ask him, he'll tell you! His trend-setting talk segment *The Highlight Reel* provides the perfect forum for Jericho to sing his own praises. There is no telling what The Ayatollah of Rock n' Rolla has in store next. One thing is for sure—he will certainly make an entrance!

HEIGHT: 6 feet (183 cm)

WEIGHT: 226 pounds (103 kg)

HOMETOWN: Winnipeg, Manitoba

SIGNATURE MOVES: Walls of Jericho, Codebreaker

Leaping ability made Jericho a lauded cruiserweight prior to his WWE career.

CONSPIRACY THEORY

Jericho has not always seen eye to eye with WWE or its Universe. He once claimed that a conspiracy perpetuated by "gelatinous tapeworms" was responsible for holding him back. He used this chip on his shoulder to add even more gold to his trophy case.

CHRISTIAN

Christian trimmed his wild hair in the early 2000s, but never lost his attitude.

A stylistic "C" is an appropriate emblem for Captain Charisma.

Christian is one of the last remaining rebels from WWE's infamous Attitude Era. Bursting onto the scene in the late '90s, the Toronto native was reeking of awesomeness while The Miz was still popping pimples in the mirror. Before he became the Captain, Christian was a decorated soldier of charisma alongside his best friend Edge. The two Canucks captivated crowds with their intrepid sense of humor and revolutionized tag team competition by adding a dose of TLC—Tables, Ladders and Chairs! Christian developed a massive following on his own. His legions of "Peeps" have helped propel him to overwhelming success. The crowning achievement on his overflowing resume is the World Heavyweight Championship, which he won for the first time in appropriate fashion, scaling a ladder with a misty-eyed Edge watching from below. As his indelible career winds down, anyone holding championship gold better be leery of this wily veteran heading down the ramp for "one more match."

HEIGHT: 6 feet, 1 inch (185 cm)

WEIGHT: 212 pounds (96 kg)

HOMETOWN:
Toronto, Ontario

SIGNATURE MOVES: Killswitch

LASTING INFLUENCE

Christian's affinity for chairs lead to the creation of the TLC Match, which later became the theme for an annual event. Aside from being a pioneer, Christian is one of most dominant Ladder Match competitors of all time. He and Edge stood victorious in Ladder Matches at *WrestleMania X-7* and *X8*.

CJ PARKER

CJ Parker's dreads celebrate all the beautiful colors of the earth.

Every day is Earth Day for CJ Parker. "The Moonchild" began his NXT career as a happy-go-lucky, free spirited Superstar. Now he is fixated on spreading his eco-friendly message. So obsessed is Parker that the NXT Universe will welcome another Ice Age if it will just shut Parker up! Parker's well-founded cause falls on deaf ears. Is it because the fans at Full Sail University do not see the big picture, or are they just put off by his exaggerated doomsday rants? This disconnect is what causes fans to treat Parker like a common pollutant. The outspoken tree-hugger doesn't care. If being an outcast serves the greater good, then that is what he will do. There is no NXT or WWE Universe without the universe, after all. He is always revving with energy (green energy, of course), so bring your A-game against Parker, or become an endangered species.

When not competing, Parker can be found parading around the ring spreading his agenda with protest signs.

HEIGHT: 6 feet, 3 inches (191 cm)

WEIGHT: 220 pounds (100 kg)

HOMETOWN: Joliet, IL

SIGNATURE MOVE: Third Eye

INTEGRITY, LOVE AND UNITY

CJ Parker was not always so self-righteous about his love for the earth. In his early days in NXT, Parker was just NXT's resident flowerchild, just staying true to himself in all his multi-colored glory.

COLIN CASSADY

Colin Cassady has the most devastating running elbow drop in the Big Apple.

Colin Cassady has all the qualities of a true New Yorker. He revels in an old fashion brawl and always has a snappy comeback for anyone's trash talk. Growing up in one of the grittiest neighborhoods of the five boroughs, Cassady honed these skills for survival. Now, he flaunts them in the hopes that he will be WWE's next breakout Superstar. With his Empire State Building-like size, there is little reason to doubt this brash youngster. As he says, "Most people spend their whole lives trying to make it big, but I, well, I was born to be big!" Cassady is never short on words, especially paired with his brash buddy, Enzo Amore. The two Big Apple brawlers put the bad mouth on their rivals, running them down with their signature taunt of "SAWFT!" Anyone who doesn't want this misspelled label better step up to this towering Superstar.

"Big Cass" is nearly seven-feet tall, and as Enzo Amore is quick to point out, "you can't teach that!"

Cassady's tights advertise the fact that he is the pride of his home borough.

HEIGHT: 6 feet, 10 inches (208 cm)
WEIGHT: 276 pounds (125 kg)
HOMETOWN: Queens, NY
SIGNATURE MOVE:
East River Crossing, Empire Elbow

MANLINESS VS OLD FASHIONED GRIT
Colin Cassady and Aiden English have blended like oil and water in NXT. The two tough guys from different eras brawled in several singles clashes while Enzo Amore was injured. When Enzo returned, the rivalry continued. The two New Yorkers targeted English's team, The Vaudevillians.

"COWBOY" BOB ORTON

Orton played up his "Cowboy" moniker, sporting an appropriate hat and vest.

The youngest WWE Universe members know "Cowboy" Bob Orton as the father of Randy Orton. Before Apex Predator first uncoiled, however, his father was producing a Hall of Fame career in WWE. The elder Orton was a trendsetter. He popularized the Superplex before it became commonplace for Superstars to utilize the ropes. He spent a large portion of his career standing with his arms folded behind "Rowdy" Roddy Piper, shooting a threatening glare at anyone who looked at the Hot Rod sideways. Orton was Piper's ace in the hole for several years, although an ill-fated swing of his cast cost Piper's team at the first *WrestleMania*. Perhaps it was karma, as Orton's need for the cast was debatable at best. The injury seemed rather convenient when Orton continued to wallop opponents with the cast. "Ace," as he was known later, left a lasting legacy, one that is still carried on today through The Viper.

HEIGHT: 6 feet, 1 inch (185 cm)

WEIGHT: 242 pounds (110 kg)

HOMETOWN: Kansas City, KS

SIGNATURE MOVE: Superplex

"Cowboy" Bob Orton's "injury" allowed him to compete with a rock hard foreign object attached to his arm.

LIKE FATHER, LIKE SON

"Cowboy" Bob Orton aided his son, Randy, during his infamous run in with Undertaker in 2005. After the youngest Orton became a Streak victim at *WrestleMania*, the father and son duo retaliated by locking Undertaker in a casket and setting it ablaze. Undertaker got revenge, however, defeating Randy in a Hell in a Cell Match and sending his father away for good.

CURTIS AXEL

When Curtis Axel grows his scruff, he bears a striking resemblance to his grandfather, The Axe.

Axel was present at the 2007 WWE Hall of Fame Induction Ceremony. He and his family accepted induction on behalf of his father, Mr. Perfect.

Curtis Axel was not just bred for sports-entertainment, you might say he had the "perfect" upbringing for a WWE Superstar. Though it took some astute mentoring from Paul Heyman, the competitor formerly known as Michael McGillicutty fully embraces his lineage. Much like a certain "electrifying" third-generation Superstar, Axel's moniker is a tribute to his father and grandfather, "Mr. Perfect" Curt Hennig and Larry "The Axe" Hennig. Though he is no longer a "Paul Heyman Guy," Axel brings the same guiding principles to the ring that won him his first Intercontinental Championship in 2013. Along with the Hennig penchant for rule-breaking, Axel combines his father's cunning with his grandfather's merciless style. This cruel streak made him the perfect partner for Ryback in 2014. Together "RybAxel" became a thorn in the side for The Usos and the rest of WWE's tag team division. Axel remains as determined as ever to carve his own legacy in WWE.

HEIGHT: 6 feet, 3 inches (191 cm)
WEIGHT: 227 pounds (103 kg)
HOMETOWN: Champlin, MN
SIGNATURE MOVES: Perfectplex

DAMIEN SANDOW

Sandow casts a disdainful look on any crass behavior or tomfoolery.

Sandow's beard is always neatly cropped to a gentleman's length.

Sandow's fashion exudes taste and an intellect one step higher than valedictorian.

Damien Sandow is the self-proclaimed "Intellectual Savior of the Masses." With a vocabulary more vast than Webster's dictionary, WWE is his lectern from which to pontificate to what he views as a sea of unwashed miscreants. It is his scholarly duty to bestow an element of dignity and class to those who have been led astray by certain unwelcome influences. Allow him to beg your indulgence for just a few moments. His profound message may be the elixir to set you on the path towards enlightenment and refinement, or you may wish to tear out your eardrums. Either way, you're welcome. When not waxing philosophical on matters of the intellect, Sandow is an esteemed competitor in the ring. The studious Superstar is pure of mind and body, so if his stately sermons do not expand your craniums, perhaps a physical schooling is in order?

HEIGHT:
6 feet, 4 inches (193 cm)

WEIGHT: 243 pounds (110 kg)

HOMETOWN:
Palo Alto, CA

SIGNATURE MOVES:
Terminus

MULTIPLICITY

Call it an identity crisis, or just incredible range as a showman—in 2014, Damien Sandow began deriding his opponents and his audience each week by playing a different character. Whether needling the hometown sports team, mocking a local celebrity, or finding a particular sensitivity, his Sandow-ized machinations always got under the skin.

DANIEL BRYAN

Daniel Bryan has rallied the WWE Universe to dream the impossible like no other Superstar in recent memory. Undersized and overlooked for much of his career, The Authority dismisses him as a "B-plus player," not capable of leading the charge as the "Face of WWE." The scrappy fireplug disagrees, as do his legions of fans who continue to sound their allegiance with deafening shouts of, "YES! YES! YES!" Bryan's catch phrase evolved from chant to a full-fledged movement that reached a crescendo at *WrestleMania 30*. Buoyed by the delirious Super Dome crowd, The Beard upended his chief tormentors, winning the WWE World Heavyweight Championship. His improbable journey took many twists and turns. The submissions specialist traveled the globe for ten years before breaking into WWE, and has spent his entire career fighting to prove himself. No matter what challenges lay ahead, the Yes! Man is ready and determined to face them.

Daniel Bryan defeated both Batista and Randy Orton at *WrestleMania 30* despite sustaining a shoulder injury in the night's opening match against Triple H.

Certain entities have tried to coerce Bryan into shaving his most distinguishable feature. Thankfully, this is one idea to which Daniel gives a defiant, "NO!"

Daniel's throwback maroon has become the identifying color for him and the Yes! Movement.

HEIGHT: 5 feet, 10 inches (178 cm)

WEIGHT: 210 pounds (95 kg)

HOMETOWN: Aberdeen, WA

SIGNATURE MOVE:
"Yes!" Lock, Running Knee

A MOVEMENT BEGINS

Daniel Bryan's lowest moment featured a silver lining. His lapse in focus caused him to lose in 18 seconds at *WrestleMania XXVIII*, but the defeat inspired fans to rally behind him. "Yes!" chants became more audible and have been gaining volume ever since.

DARREN YOUNG

Darren Young added the pick during his Primetime Player days to complete his million dollar style.

Darren Young became a household name as part of the Primetime Players. With fellow NXT alum Titus O'Neil as his ally, the flashy duo brought some show time swagger to the tag team ranks. Despite being on the cocky side, supporters began to echo their cause, swaying along with them to the rallying cry, "Millions of dollars! Millions of dollars!" Unfortunately, PTP fell short of this lofty goal. O'Neil grew frustrated and severed the partnership, blindsiding Young with a punishing cheap shot. Now on his own, Darren Young still prides himself in his tireless dedication. "Mr. No Days Off" is not looking back, despite lingering dissention with his ex-partner. He just keeps on churning forward, seizing each day as an opportunity to live up to his boastful nickname. So far, no one can question his devotion. Darren Young has the fortitude to face whatever challenges lie in his path.

HEIGHT: 6 feet, 1 inch (185 cm)
WEIGHT: 239 pounds (108 kg)
HOMETOWN: Miami, FL
SIGNATURE MOVES: Gut Check

STRENGTH IN NUMBERS

Darren Young impressed on the first season of *NXT*. Wade Barrett emerged as the season's winner, but that did not stop Young and the entire cast from leaving their mark. The classmates banded together like a tribe of hooligans and made life miserable for John Cena and other top Superstars.

DAVID OTUNGA

From the classroom to the courtroom, to the most exclusive Hollywood circles, David Otunga is an A-list player. He knows it, too. Since WWE cameras first cast their lenses over his chiseled physique on *NXT* Season 1, Otunga has carried himself like a man with everything going for him. He shares the same academic clout as the 44th President of the United States. He is built like The Terminator and is married to a world famous celebrity starlet. Object to those Superstar credentials, and you'll be swiftly overruled. Sustained success, however, is a different story. The facts state that Otunga's in-ring career has been uneven thus far. Nevertheless, his services remain in high demand. The prized litigator has helped several WWE Superstars and executives settle their scores by the letter of the law. As for a verdict on Otunga's World Title hopes, the jury is still out.

Otunga's trunks bear the maroon color of his alma mater, Harvard.

Otunga flexes his shredded muscles for the crowd before his matches.

HEIGHT: 6 feet (183 cm)

WEIGHT: 229 pounds (104 kg)

HOMETOWN: Hollywood, CA

SUPERSTAR COUNCEL

David Otunga is a pricy attorney, not a problem for Alberto Del Rio. The Mexican Aristocrat enlisted Otunga to get a leg up on Sheamus in their rivalry for the World Heavyweight Championship. Otunga succeeded in getting Sheamus's Brogue Kick banned, but the ruling was overturned days later. Whether he still charged Alberto full price for his services is unknown.

DEAN AMBROSE

Dean Ambrose's perpetual sneer exudes bad intentions. You never know what kind of dark thoughts are swimming through his head.

Dean Ambrose was once the maniacal mouthpiece of The Shield. Flanked by Roman Reigns and Seth Rollins, Ambrose promised and helped deliver a swift brand of justice to all who had it coming. Now that the Hounds of Justice are no more, Ambrose has not stopped living on the lunatic fringe. If anything, he has danced even closer to the edge of madness. As unstable as ever, his next move is anyone's guess, but all indications are that it will not be for the faint of heart. Inflicting and sustaining damage is his specialty, and victory is merely a byproduct. The more dangerous and volatile the environment, the more at peace Ambrose seems to be. His words are cryptic. His actions are impulsive. Ambrose is a one-man hornet's nest, and now that he is on his own, the entire WWE locker room better be ready to feel his sting.

Since abandoning his black Shield flak jacket, Ambrose has gone to a gritty street look.

HEIGHT: 6 feet, 4 inches (193 cm)

WEIGHT: 225 pounds (102 kg)

HOMETOWN: Cincinnati, OH

SIGNATURE MOVE: Dirty Deeds

UNITED STATES OF AMBROSE

Dean Ambrose was the first member of The Shield to win a singles title. At *Extreme Rules 2013*, he upended Kofi Kingston for the United States Championship. The Lunatic Fringe held onto the title for 351 days until placed in a 20-Man Battle Royal by Triple H. In an unwinnable situation, Ambrose nearly succeeded, being the last Superstar eliminated.

DEVIN TAYLOR

Devin Taylor's good looks attracted the attention of advertisers prior to her NXT career. She was featured in national print ads before trying out sports-entertainment.

Devin Taylor delights the NXT Universe each week by getting the inside scoop on all the action featuring the WWE Superstars of the future. Taylor has competed in the ring before, first trying her hand at NXT competition in June 2014. She asserted herself well enough to give any NXT Diva second thoughts about getting on her bad side. She is most in her element, however, with her hand firmly wrapped around a microphone. Devin Taylor has many skills, but her nose for a good story makes her a natural for the broadcast team. Since making her debut as an interviewer, she has tracked down a wide variety of NXT stars backstage, from the overexcited Bayley to a man with a NXT Championship on his resume, Adrian Neville.

HEIGHT: 5 feet, 4 inches (163 cm)
HOMETOWN: Temecula, CA

SCHOLAR ATHLETE

Devin Taylor has a degree in Broadcast Journalism from Loyala Maramount University. She also had an impressive soccer career, earning scholar-athlete honors and even competing in the Youth World Cup. Perhaps we have not seen the last of Taylor in the ring after all?

DIAMOND DALLAS PAGE

For a man who did not begin competing in matches until his mid-thirties, Diamond Dallas Page put together a career worthy of a "self high five." DDP was known for his dangerous finisher, the Diamond Cutter, and the signature hand gesture alerting fans that it was coming. He was one of the most revered Superstars in the history of WCW. He won the World Championship for WWE's competition and was responsible for bringing NBA legend Karl Malone to the ring for some well-publicized crossover matches. When Page came to WWE, he wasted no time calling out the biggest dog in the yard, Undertaker. Page played head games, stalking The Deadman's wife and igniting a simmering rivalry. Though Undertaker got the better of him, that summer he paired with fellow WCW invader Kanyon to win tag team hardware. Page won his lone *WrestleMania* match, teaching Christian a lesson in positivity in the process.

Diamond Dallas Page was a celebrated talker. He put the icing on his speeches by high fiving one hand with the other hand.

DDP had some of the coolest leather vests, with lightning bolts cascading down each side.

HEIGHT: 6 feet, 5 inches (196 cm)

WEIGHT: 248 pounds (112 kg)

HOMETOWN: The Jersey Shore

SIGNATURE MOVE: Diamond Cutter

DOWNWARD DOG PAGE

Today, DDP continues to be an asset to sports-entertainment. His DDP Yoga is popular with several Superstars. Chris Jericho has been a big proponent for the program and Jake "The Snake" Roberts credits Page for turning his life around. DDP inducted Roberts into the Hall of Fame in 2014.

DIEGO

This headwear is synonymous with the bullfighters of Plaza de Toros. Its bulbs are symbolic of a bull's horns.

¡Olé! Outside of Plaza De Toros, Los Matadores once existed purely in myth, with tales of their bravery stretching far and wide. Many matadors have donned the traje de luces, with conquests of fame and fortune on their minds. Many paid the ultimate price for their machismo. Others simply vanished, leaving only their specter in the dusty bullfighting rings housing the mighty toros. Los Matadores rose above them all, solidifying a permanent place in toreador folklore before they vanished. Now, their valiant crusade for victory and spoils is reborn in a different kind of ring. Diego thrills the WWE Universe by locking horns with WWE's most dangerous duos alongside his masked compadre, Fernando. Like any good matadors, they become one with the bull, and even bring one to the ring in the form of El Torito.

Short jacket with reflective gold threads looks majestic and allows for quick, decisive movement of the arms.

HEIGHT: 5 feet, 10 inches (178 cm)

WEIGHT: 215 pounds (98 kg)

HOMETOWN: Plaza De Toros

Knee-length tights allow for seamless transition from bullfighting to WWE.

THE GRANDEST STAGE

In their first year of tag team competition, Los Matadores found themselves opening the grandest show on the WWE calendar. Though they failed to conquer three other teams to claim tag team gold, they fought with great courage. Think twice before locking horns with Diego and Fernando.

DOINK THE CLOWN

Depending how you feel about clowns, Doink's painted face either conjures memories of balloon animals and card tricks or terrifying nightmares.

In the mid-'90s, Doink gave the WWE Superstars and fans a severe case of coulrophobia, better known as "fear of clowns." His malicious pranks played into people's irrational trepidation associated with jesting circus performers. Doink reveled in his wicked ways, laughing like mad behind his white make-up. There seemed no end to his trickery. He even seemed to multiply at *WrestleMania IX*. His opponent, Crush, was not amused to contend with two Doinks at the same time! Over time, the notorious joker became more lighthearted. Villains such as Jerry "The King" Lawler started taking the brunt of his gags, and fans stopped being freaked out when circus music engulfed the arena. Doink made clownery so cool, in fact, that he brought in miniature sidekicks Dink, Pink, and Wink to get even more laughs at The King's expense. Years later, Doink still pops up occasionally like a jack-in-the-box, full of surprises.

Doink wore a loud combination of blue, red, and yellow, often accented with stars or a gaudy green tie. His attire was perfect for competition or for juggling fruit.

HEIGHT:
5 feet, 10 inches (178 cm)

WEIGHT: 243 pounds (110 kg)

SIGNATURE MOVE:
The Stump Puller,
The Whoopie Cushion

IMPOSTERS

Many Superstars have impersonated Doink for their own personal gain. Chris Jericho donned the clown suit for a surprise attack on William Regal in 2001. Days later at *WrestleMania X-Seven*, the real thing emerged to show Y2J how it was done. He entered the Gimmick Battle Royal and racked up two eliminations before being tossed.

DOLPH ZIGGLER

Shades of Ric Flair, Dolph's signature blonde hair is always slicked to perfection.

Dolph Ziggler is here to steal the show...and your girlfriend too. Since he first introduced himself to WWE, Dolph has brought a cocksure attitude to the ring to go with his South Beach abdominals and luminous platinum hair. With a nickname like "The Showoff," confidence has never been a problem. Neither has his amazing athleticism. The skills he crafted while setting amateur records have served him well on the big time WWE stage. The day after a historic *WrestleMania 29*, Dolph sent the *Raw* crowd into delirium, cashing in his title shot on Alberto Del Rio and turning the Money in the Bank spotlight onto his tanned shoulders. Ziggler shined as the center of attention, completing a full transition to fan favorite. Though his recent record has been far from perfect, it is only a matter of time before Dolph shows the world what he is made of once again.

HEIGHT: 6 feet (183 cm)

WEIGHT: 213 pounds (97 kg)

HOMETOWN: Hollywood, FL

SIGNATURE MOVES:
Zig Zag

NICKNAME:
The Showoff

Dolph's bold wardrobe includes zebra skin patterns, hot pink, bright purple, and other loud color combos.

Dolph excels in the ring, and looks good doing it with his sculpted physique.

LADIES' MAN

Dolph used his good looks to woo *SmackDown* General Manager Vickie Guerrero. Their relationship toed the lines of professional decency, as Dolph used the smitten cougar to advance his career. Later on, he found a younger squeeze, AJ Lee. Along with their enforcer, Big E, the devilish AJ provided ringside assistance for her blonde beau.

DON MURACO

Don Muraco did not care much for the rules. The arrogant one known as "Magnificent Muraco" tormented WWE's most revered heroes throughout the 1980s. Though fans disparaged him with chants of "Beach Bum," Muraco was one of the most prolific competitors of his time and one of the most definitive Intercontinental Champions, holding the prize for a combined eighteen months over two separate reigns. During this time, his hostile and epic encounters with Pedro Morales added prestige to the newly minted title. Muraco was such a hot commodity that he was managed by four different WWE Hall of Famers: The Grand Wizard, Captain Lou Albano, Mr. Fuji, and Superstar Billy Graham. With Fuji, he showed his acting chops in the popular parody vignette, "Fuji Vice." Muraco won over fans later in his career—still not quite the People's Champ—but he was the first Superstar to be called "The Rock."

HEIGHT: 6 feet, 3 inches (191 cm)

WEIGHT: 275 pounds (125 kg)

HOMETOWN: Sunset Beach, HI

Don Muraco's solid build is what led fans to nickname him "The Rock." He often wore tie-dye while associated with Superstar Billy Graham.

DON THE FIRST

Nineteen Superstars have been crowned King of the Ring in the tournament's history. The list includes Stone Cold Steve Austin, Bret Hart, Randy Savage, and other greats. Only Muraco, however, can claim to be the first. Muraco won the inaugural tournament in 1985.

DUSTY RHODES

Dusty Rhodes's Bionic Elbow has rained down on the foreheads of Hall of Famers such as Harley Race and Superstar Billy Graham.

Dusty Rhodes is the proud papa of two WWE standouts, Stardust and Goldust. Long before Goldust caked on his first gob of gold paint however, Dusty laid the groundwork for the Rhodes family legacy. The "son of a plumber" embraced his blue collar upbringing. His uphill climb to stardom in the NWA was relatable to audiences up and down the east coast, and the man with a preacher's soul talked them into the building with a flourish far ahead of his time. He did not have the physique of a comic book hero or an encyclopedia of holds and he never saw the view from top rope. But Dusty still captivated crowds, not just filling, but keeping, rear-ends on the edges of seats. He was a Hall of Famer long before he first busted a move in WWE wearing yellow polka dots, and his influence is still felt today.

Dusty Rhodes shared a hair color with Ric Flair, but not much else. Dusty clashed with the high-rolling Four Horsemen leader in one of the most heated rivalries of the 1980s.

HEIGHT:
6 feet, 2 inches (188 cm)

WEIGHT: 275 pounds (125 kg)

HOMETOWN:
Austin, TX

SIGNATURE MOVE:
Bionic Elbow

FATHER KNOWS BEST

Dusty still returns on occasion, often to help his boys in times of need. In 2013, he stood by the two brothers as they fought for their careers against The Shield. Not only did they save their jobs but they captured the Tag Team Titles soon after. The apples clearly did not fall far from the tree!

EARTHQUAKE

Earthquake covered his massive proportions with a singlet bearing his name and readings from a seismograph.

Earthquake shook the terrain in WWE throughout the early 1990s. The seismic heavyweight inflicted damage on both Ultimate Warrior and Hulk Hogan within one year of competing. Hogan even sustained broken ribs due to an attack from the Canadian colossus. Although Hulk got his revenge, Earthquake's fury was far from settled. His most dastardly act came at the expense of Jake "The Snake" Roberts. Earthquake dropped his nearly 500 pound body on the bag containing Damien, putting an end to Robert's beloved reptile. If one natural disaster was not enough, Earthquake teamed with Typhoon. One of the heaviest teams in history, the two behemoths won the Tag Team Titles. The shockwaves from Earthquake's destructive deeds eventually wore off. By the time the dust settled on his WWE career, fans became fond of him. He came back to ping the Richter scale one more time at *WrestleMania X-Seven* for the Gimmick Battle Royal in 2001.

Earthquake finished off opponents by crushing them under his gigantic hindquarters.

HEIGHT: 6 feet, 7 inches (201 cm)

WEIGHT: 248 pounds (112 kg)

HOMETOWN: Vancouver, British Columbia

SIGNATURE MOVE: Earthquake Splash

SUMO CHALLENGE

Earthquake was a noted sumo wrestler before getting into sports-entertainment. This made him a natural rival for Yokozuna. Though the Japanese Hall of Famer is remembered more for his sumo prowess, Earthquake actually beat him in their one Sumo Match.

EDDIE GUERRERO

Eddie Guerrero was so charming that his blatant chicanery in the ring only warmed the hearts of those who caught him red-handed. Sure, he would lie, cheat, and steal... but at least he was honest about it! Plus, who can resist that trademark grin that said, "What? Who, me?" Behind this magnetic exterior, however, lived a performer of incredible versatility who harbored an insatiable passion for entertainment. Eddie could make the WWE Universe hate him, love him, or wonder where they stood, often in the same night. He was athletic enough to match Rey Mysterio leap for leap one week, then lock up with the monstrous Brock Lesnar the next. His crowning achievement came against Lesnar when his breathtaking Frog Splash sealed his first and only reign as WWE Champion.

At *WrestleMania XX*, Eddie foiled Kurt Angle's Ankle Lock attempt by loosening his bootstraps when the gold medalist was not looking.

HEIGHT: 5 feet, 8 inches (173 cm)

WEIGHT: 220 pounds (100 kg)

HOMETOWN: El Paso, TX

SIGNATURE MOVE: Frog Splash

LATINO HEAT

Eddie Guerrero oozed charisma from the very beginning in WWE. He won Chyna's heart and racked up several championships. Distracted referees were none the wiser when he pounded on a chair and laid flat on the mat, causing a disqualification for his opponent.

EDEN

Eden is a natural fit for sports-entertainment. She worked as a TV news reporter in Michigan for two years, the state where she earned her college degree. From there, she branched out into the world of modeling. Lucky for those of us with functioning retinas, the beautiful bombshell was featured in several ads for Budweiser, KFC, and *Maxim* Magazine. Now, she is entrenched in NXT, proving herself as a well-spoken personality. Eden is usually found conducting her ring announcing duties. She is also outspoken on social media and wwe.com. She keeps her Twitter account active with her unique slant on WWE's latest developments. She has also allowed WWE cameras to get a glimpse of her personal life. Fans have gotten to see her interact with various Superstars outside the ring, including her close encounters with Stardust, who seems to be one of her favorite competitors.

While classified as a NXT announcer, Eden has also wielded a microphone on *SmackDown* and *WWE Main Event*.

HEIGHT: 5 feet, 5 inches (165 cm)

HOMETOWN: Ann Arbor, MI

BLOGGING BEAUTY

Eden's video blog on wwe.com has shown all sides of this captivating Diva. Eden has revealed everything from her wardrobe to her favorite activities, pet peeves, and more.

EDGE

Edge's talk show *The Cutting Edge* was the perfect forum for his outspoken wit on the microphone.

Edge became one of the greatest tag team competitors of all time before Spearing his way into singles competition. It was clear that no measure was too extreme to fulfill his destiny of becoming WWE Champion. He transformed into the Rated-R Superstar, showcasing his sleazy side and becoming one of the most despised villains of the modern era. His cutthroat tactics and venomous remarks did not earn him too many friends, but they did earn him the championship he desperately coveted. Edge was a mainstay title picture for several years until injury forced his untimely retirement. He rode off into the sunset with eleven World Championships and zero regrets. Now, when "You Think You Know Me" echoes off the rafters, the WWE Universe greets him with a warm ovation out of respect for his Hall of Fame career.

HEIGHT: 6 feet, 5 inches (196 cm)

WEIGHT: 241 pounds (109 kg)

HOMETOWN: Toronto, Ontario

SIGNATURE MOVE: Spear

Edge's rock star appearance is part of what made him the perfect foil for the clean cut John Cena.

EDGE & CHRISTIAN

As the architects of the Tables, Ladders & Chairs Match, this legendary tandem revolutionized Tag Team competition in WWE, racking up fourteen Tag Team Titles before splitting.

EL TORITO

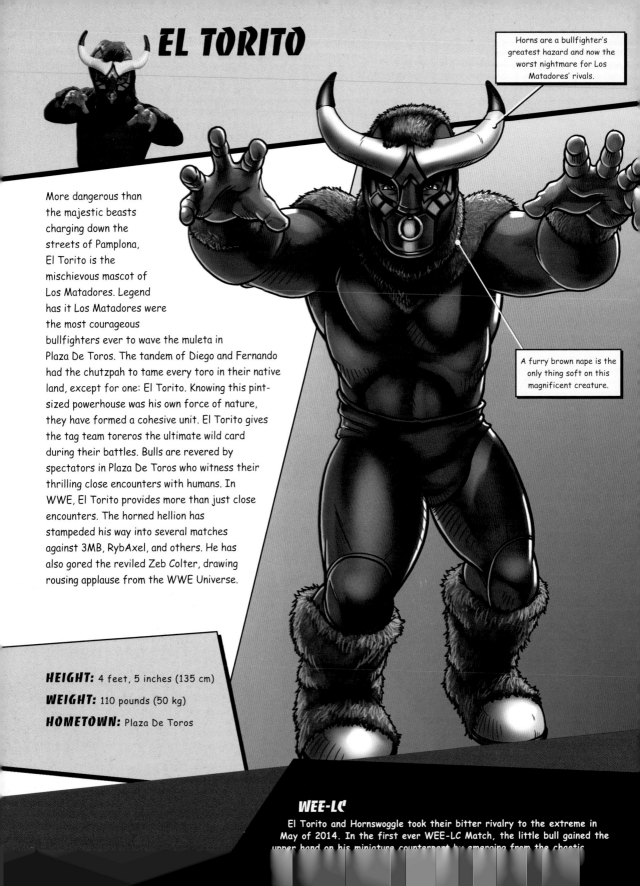

Horns are a bullfighter's greatest hazard and now the worst nightmare for Los Matadores' rivals.

More dangerous than the majestic beasts charging down the streets of Pamplona, El Torito is the mischievous mascot of Los Matadores. Legend has it Los Matadores were the most courageous bullfighters ever to wave the muleta in Plaza De Toros. The tandem of Diego and Fernando had the chutzpah to tame every toro in their native land, except for one: El Torito. Knowing this pint-sized powerhouse was his own force of nature, they have formed a cohesive unit. El Torito gives the tag team toreros the ultimate wild card during their battles. Bulls are revered by spectators in Plaza De Toros who witness their thrilling close encounters with humans. In WWE, El Torito provides more than just close encounters. The horned hellion has stampeded his way into several matches against 3MB, RybAxel, and others. He has also gored the reviled Zeb Colter, drawing rousing applause from the WWE Universe.

A furry brown nape is the only thing soft on this magnificent creature.

HEIGHT: 4 feet, 5 inches (135 cm)
WEIGHT: 110 pounds (50 kg)
HOMETOWN: Plaza De Toros

WEE-LC

El Torito and Hornswoggle took their bitter rivalry to the extreme in May of 2014. In the first ever WEE-LC Match, the little bull gained the upper hand on his miniature counterpart by emerging from the chaotic

EMMA

Emma is a free-spirited Diva from "down under" and the first ever Aussie female to ever grace WWE television. With a quirky confidence and carefree demeanor, her #EMMAlution continues to unfold before our eyes with each #EMMAtaining performance. Emma's unique form of self expression is confusing to many, but she is not seeking "10" signs from any snooty dance aficionados. She is here to win, and her moves are a simple celebration of that. At this rate, Emma will have a lot to celebrate in her career. More than just a dancing queen, she boasts a furious arsenal of #EMMAzing tactical maneuvers such as the Dil-Emma, Emmamite Sandwich, and the Emma Lock finisher. It was this deadly submission hold that finished off fellow dancer Summer Rae in her *Raw* debut. This strong start sent a statement to the rest of the Divas that they have company in pursuit of the butterfly title.

Want to join in Emma's victory celebration? Just pop the imaginary bubbles!

A pink Diva Cobra lurks in Emma's boots for mixed tag matches with Santino.

HEIGHT:
5 feet, 5 inches (165 cm)

HOMETOWN:
Melbourne, Australia

SIGNATURE MOVE:
Emma Lock

SNAKE CHARMER

Emma's bold performances quickly caught the eye of Santino Marella. Both he and his cobra seemed smitten with the lovely Diva, but it was not love at first cannoli for Emma. A series of awkward interactions and comical mistiming has left the lines of their relationship blurry.

ENZO AMORE

Enzo Amore looks like the baddest dude on the Jersey Shore with his spiked Mohawk, thick chain, and abundance of ink.

Enzo Amore grew up in the shadow of Manhattan. With the personality of a walking can of Red Bull, he can talk enough trash in a New York minute to force his opponents into a mental tailspin, and bust a few rhymes to boot. If you think he is all talk and no show, FUH-GE-DUH-BAH-DIT! Enzo competes with the same ferocity that he jaws at his rivals. He may be a bit small for a NXT Superstar, but it is not the size of the dog in the fight. It is the size of the fight in the dog, and Enzo has bite to match his bark. He may be a bit cocky, but there is one thing he is not—"SAFWT!" Enzo's trademark verbal barb may not win him any spelling bees, but it gets the point across. If you don't like it, do somethin' about it!

SAWFT t-shirt: 100% cotton, 0% rotten

HEIGHT: 5 feet, 11 inches (180 cm)

WEIGHT: 200 pounds (91 kg)

HOMETOWN: Hackensack, NJ

BADA-BOOM, REALEST GUYS IN THE ROOM!

Enzo Amore aligned with brash New Yorker Colin Cassady in 2013. The smack talking duo was known for speaking their minds no matter who was listening. When Enzo missed eight months with a broken leg, they picked up right where they left off, with NXT fans chanting, "Welcome back!"

ERICK ROWAN

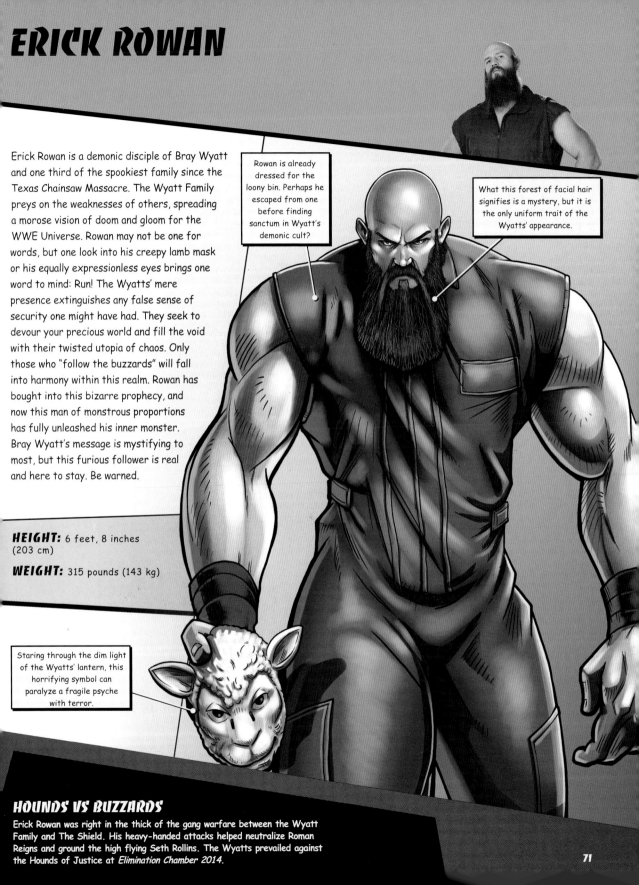

Erick Rowan is a demonic disciple of Bray Wyatt and one third of the spookiest family since the Texas Chainsaw Massacre. The Wyatt Family preys on the weaknesses of others, spreading a morose vision of doom and gloom for the WWE Universe. Rowan may not be one for words, but one look into his creepy lamb mask or his equally expressionless eyes brings one word to mind: Run! The Wyatts' mere presence extinguishes any false sense of security one might have had. They seek to devour your precious world and fill the void with their twisted utopia of chaos. Only those who "follow the buzzards" will fall into harmony within this realm. Rowan has bought into this bizarre prophecy, and now this man of monstrous proportions has fully unleashed his inner monster. Bray Wyatt's message is mystifying to most, but this furious follower is real and here to stay. Be warned.

Rowan is already dressed for the loony bin. Perhaps he escaped from one before finding sanctum in Wyatt's demonic cult?

What this forest of facial hair signifies is a mystery, but it is the only uniform trait of the Wyatts' appearance.

HEIGHT: 6 feet, 8 inches (203 cm)

WEIGHT: 315 pounds (143 kg)

Staring through the dim light of the Wyatts' lantern, this horrifying symbol can paralyze a fragile psyche with terror.

HOUNDS VS BUZZARDS

Erick Rowan was right in the thick of the gang warfare between the Wyatt Family and The Shield. His heavy-handed attacks helped neutralize Roman Reigns and ground the high flying Seth Rollins. The Wyatts prevailed against the Hounds of Justice at *Elimination Chamber 2014*.

EVA MARIE

Eva Marie's first statement as a "newbie" Diva in WWE was her fire engine hair and matching crimson ensemble, but this femme fatale is blazing in more ways than just her favorite color. First turning heads as a successful model, Eva Marie decided she was too raucous for the runway. She traded in her high heels for ring boots and set herself on a course to light up the WWE scene. In her short time as a Diva, she has proven to have a malicious mind and a sharp set of claws. She slapped Jerry Lawler across the face in her *Raw* debut and has since stepped on the toes of some veteran Divas. Natalya took exception to the brazen bombshell. The two have tussled on *Total Divas* and in the ring. With so much future ahead of Eva Marie, red means "go" for this defiant young Diva.

Eva Marie's fiery hue stands out like a beacon of danger for her opponents.

Eva Marie is decked in gleaming red from head to toe like a Phoenix rising from the ashes.

HEIGHT:
5 feet, 8 inches (173 cm)

HOMETOWN: Concord, CA

RISKY BUSINESS

Eva Marie vied for a position as Fandango's dance partner on an episode of *Total Divas*. The bold move backfired when Stephanie McMahon found out she had no dancing experience and read the newbie the riot act. While ill-advised, Eva's risk proved what lengths she will go to make it in WWE.

EVE TORRES

Eve was one of few Divas known to venture to the top turnbuckle for a majestic Moonsault.

Whether dressed for the ring or administrative duties, Eve projected the same look—classy, yet stunning.

Eve could do it all. A stunning beauty with a sharp intellect, Eve used her multifaceted skill set to her advantage over an impressive five year career in WWE. Whether as a dancer, competitor, or no-nonsense business woman, the well-rounded Diva was a force to be reckoned with. Eve has extensive training in Jiu-Jitsu, making her the most likely Diva to break both your heart and your fibula at one time. She used her training, fitness, and flexibility to earn three Divas Championships. She was the first Diva Search winner to hold the coveted title. Fans gravitated toward her, but Eve could be conniving. She toyed with Zack Ryder's emotions and curried favor with the two-faced John Laurinaitis to gain political power within WWE. Still, Eve will be remembered as a pure competitor. Since the inception of the Diva's Title, she is one of the finest champions to hold the prize.

HEIGHT: 5 feet, 8 inches (173 cm)

HOMETOWN: Denver, CO

SIGNATURE MOVE: Moonsault

POSITION'S HELD:
Executive Administrator to *Raw* & *SmackDown* GM John Laurinaitis, Assistant to the *SmackDown* General Manager

GRANDEST SABOTAGE

Eve was embroiled in a power struggle between rival GMs Teddy Long and John Laurinaitis in 2012. Eve flew Team Teddy's flag at *WrestleMania XXVIII*, but was in Big Johnny's pocket the whole time. She kicked Zack Ryder below the belt, betraying her team and swaying the power balance over to Laurinaitis.

FANDANGO

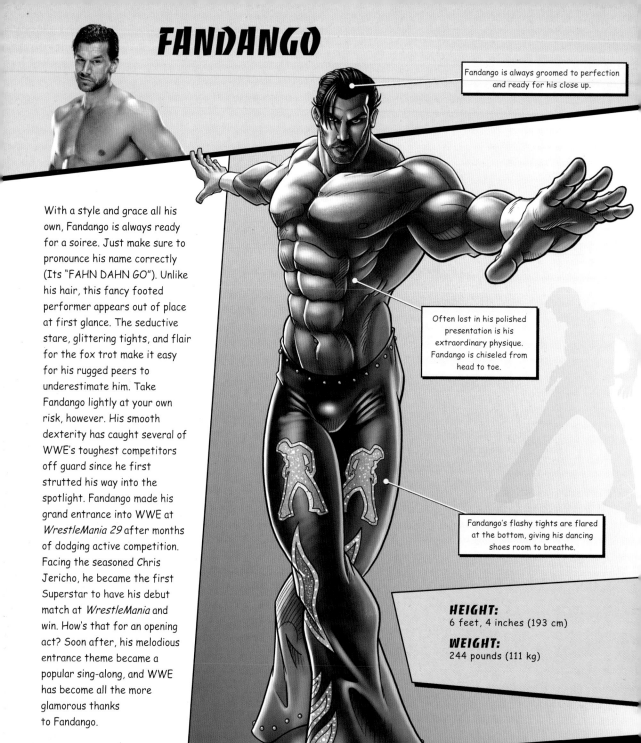

Fandango is always groomed to perfection and ready for his close up.

With a style and grace all his own, Fandango is always ready for a soiree. Just make sure to pronounce his name correctly (Its "FAHN DAHN GO"). Unlike his hair, this fancy footed performer appears out of place at first glance. The seductive stare, glittering tights, and flair for the fox trot make it easy for his rugged peers to underestimate him. Take Fandango lightly at your own risk, however. His smooth dexterity has caught several of WWE's toughest competitors off guard since he first strutted his way into the spotlight. Fandango made his grand entrance into WWE at *WrestleMania 29* after months of dodging active competition. Facing the seasoned Chris Jericho, he became the first Superstar to have his debut match at *WrestleMania* and win. How's that for an opening act? Soon after, his melodious entrance theme became a popular sing-along, and WWE has become all the more glamorous thanks to Fandango.

Often lost in his polished presentation is his extraordinary physique. Fandango is chiseled from head to toe.

Fandango's flashy tights are flared at the bottom, giving his dancing shoes room to breathe.

HEIGHT:
6 feet, 4 inches (193 cm)

WEIGHT:
244 pounds (111 kg)

#DUMPED

For the first part of his career, Fandango twirled his way to the ring with the elegant Summer Rae by his side. He seemed content with the leggy blonde but in the midst of a slump he dropped a Twitter bombshell. Fandango kicked Summer Rae to the curb over social media in favor of Layla. As karma would have it, today neither Diva wants anything to do with this tangoing two-timer.

FERNANDO

Fernando is one of two matadors to rise to the mythical heights only dreamed of by the bullfighting brethren of Plaza De Toros. The other is Diego and together they have reemerged in WWE as Los Matadores. The daring duo is armed with bravado and skills sharpened by treacherous encounters with the meanest toros in Spain. Their quest is to vault to the top of WWE's tag team ranks. They left their blood and sweat in Plaza De Toros, but they brought one important component with them to WWE: El Torito. This mighty little bull is notorious for sticking his horns into their matchups and evening the score with troublesome meddlers such as Hornswoggle and Zeb Colter. The combined strength of these two toreros and their stampeding mascot should make even the biggest beasts in WWE leery of charging into the ring. Fernando and Diego's ascension has just begun. Ole!

HEIGHT: 6 feet (183 cm)
WEIGHT: 217 pounds (98 kg)
HOMETOWN: Plaza De Toros

Most bullfighters want their faces seen, but Los Matadores conceal their identities for added mystique.

Getting dressed is its own ritual for Fernando and reflective gold sequins are the key to a majestic appearance.

The matador's traditional knee high socks are specially tailored from pink silk.

NOSOTROS, EL PUEBLO

Los Matadores got off to a roaring start on pay-per-view. Zeb Colter's Real Americans may not appreciate the foreigners' arrival in the USA, but they must give credit where it is due. In their first primetime clash at *Hell in a Cell*, the masked matadors scored a victory over Swagger and Cesaro.

FINLAY

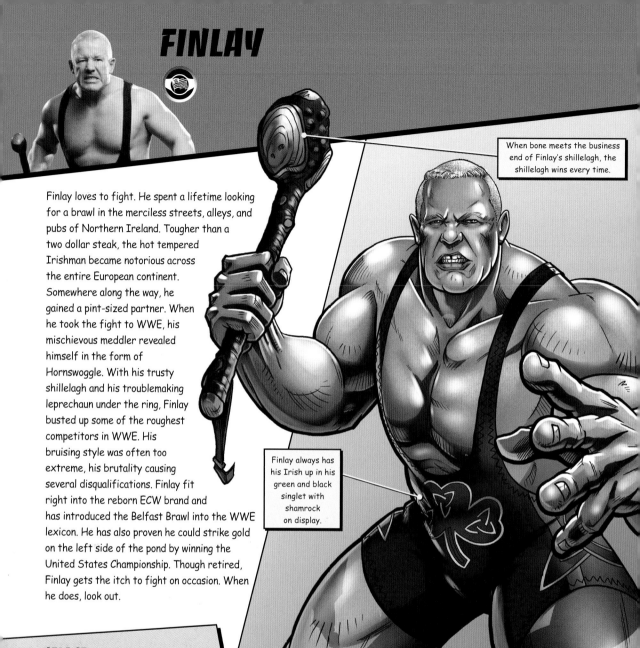

When bone meets the business end of Finlay's shillelagh, the shillelagh wins every time.

Finlay loves to fight. He spent a lifetime looking for a brawl in the merciless streets, alleys, and pubs of Northern Ireland. Tougher than a two dollar steak, the hot tempered Irishman became notorious across the entire European continent. Somewhere along the way, he gained a pint-sized partner. When he took the fight to WWE, his mischievous meddler revealed himself in the form of Hornswoggle. With his trusty shillelagh and his troublemaking leprechaun under the ring, Finlay busted up some of the roughest competitors in WWE. His bruising style was often too extreme, his brutality causing several disqualifications. Finlay fit right into the reborn ECW brand and has introduced the Belfast Brawl into the WWE lexicon. He has also proven he could strike gold on the left side of the pond by winning the United States Championship. Though retired, Finlay gets the itch to fight on occasion. When he does, look out.

Finlay always has his Irish up in his green and black singlet with shamrock on display.

HEIGHT:
6 feet, 2 inches (188 cm)

WEIGHT: 233 pounds (106 kg)

HOMETOWN:
Belfast, Northern Ireland

SIGNATURE MOVE:
Celtic Cross

BELFAST BRAWL

When JBL began nosing around in Finlay's personal life in 2008, the bruising Irishman took the arrogant loudmouth to task in a Belfast Brawl. Though JBL got the victory at *Wrestle Mania XXIV*, Finlay's hard-hitting performance served as a warning to anyone thinking about crossing him.

FINN BALOR

In his sports-entertainment career, Balor has been known to transform himself for special occasions, using body paint to unleash the perfect alter ego.

A swirling tempest of intrigue engulfs the NXT landscape, and at the eye of the storm stands Finn Balor. Over a 15-year odyssey, Balor has traversed every sports-entertainment stop on the globe except for the one with the brightest stage: WWE. Is the conqueror formerly known the world over as Prince Devitt ready for the WWE spotlight? The better question may be, is WWE ready for him? Balor spent eight years on the pressure-packed, unforgiving canvas of New Japan Pro Wrestling. While there, he held the promotion's IWGP Junior Heavyweight Championship, a deeply respected title, for 14 months. And he did it with flair. Balor's theatrical prowess speaks to his love of comic book heroes and villains. With a new moniker derived from warriors and demons of Gaelic mythology, he can be friend or foe. Either way, the future is indeed now.

HEIGHT: 5 feet, 11 inches (180 cm)

WEIGHT: 189 pounds (86 kg)

HOMETOWN: Bray, County Wicklow, Ireland

SIGNATURE MOVES: Bloody Sunday, Balor's Throne, Balor's End

INTERNATIONAL STARS ALIGN

Finn Balor wasted no time making his presence known in NXT. Watching fellow newcomer Hideo Itami stand up to repeated attacks from The Ascension, the international star emerged to even the odds and introduce himself to his new home in the process.

FREDDIE BLASSIE

This notorious foreign object came in handy for two foreigners at the first *WrestleMania*. Blassie passed the cane to Iron Sheik, who used it to nail Barry Windham and seal the victory for the team.

Freddie Blassie's gaudy suits are just one reason he considered himself the "Hollywood Fashion Plate."

Listen you pencil-necked geeks! "Classy" Freddie Blassie is the most despised man in the history of sports-entertainment. Many fans are too young to remember the self-proclaimed "Hollywood Fashion Plate" berating crowds with his signature taunt. Blassie passed on when John Cena was still a promising rookie. However, his influence has endured. Blassie laid the blueprint for villainy as both a competitor and manager. He was reviled and feared during his active years. His penchant for biting opponents and other heinous tactics earned him disdain and caused dangerous riots. As a manager, he had a way of insulting crowds that cut down to the bone. Boos echoed off the rafters as he extolled his beefed up stable of evildoers. Blassie reveled in the hatred, and for his vile acts of treachery the WWE Universe owes him two words—thank you. Without villains, there are no heroes. Blassie made us believe in our heroes.

HEIGHT: 5 feet, 10 inches (178 cm)

WEIGHT: 220 pounds (100 kg)

HOMETOWN: St. Louis, MO

SIGNATURE MOVE: Stomach Claw

SUPERSTARS MANAGED:
High Chief Peter Maivia, Jesse Ventura, Mr. Fuji, Hulk Hogan, George "The Animal" Steele, Iron Sheik, Nikolai Volkoff

BEFORE THE MANIA

Even one of WWE's most revered heroes got his start as one of Blassie's henchman. Few remember, but Blassie guided Hulk Hogan during his early years. Despite these wrongdoings, Hogan revealed his true colors a few years later. Hulkamania began running wild when Hogan dropped his leg over another Blassie client, Iron Sheik.

GEORGE "THE ANIMAL" STEELE

Other Superstars have been nicknamed "The Animal," but George "The Animal" Steele took originality to another level. Unique, peculiar, and slightly terrifying, George Steele broke the mold for a WWE Superstar. His appearance unnerved opponents. For starters, his tongue was green, which did not make his menacing array of facial expressions any easier on the eyes. Neither did his wooly coat of body hair. George Steele may have eaten his opponents for lunch, had he not satiated his hunger by devouring the turnbuckles. Whether this bizarre dietary choice is related to his lime-colored tongue remains unexplained. The Animal displayed a soft side when he became infatuated with the lovely Miss Elizabeth. His affectionate displays toward his leading lady infuriated Randy Savage. Steele's affable brand of chivalry delighted crowds. Fans cheered this unusual and compelling Superstar right up to his Hall of Fame induction.

Steele's bizarre green tongue made even the bravest opponents leery of a close encounter with The Animal.

George Steele's famous body hair was part of what made him one of WWE's most recognizable figures.

HEIGHT:
6 feet, 1 inch (185 cm)

WEIGHT: 275 pounds (125 kg)

HOMETOWN: Detroit, MI

SIGNATURE MOVE: Flying Hammerlock

THE ANIMAL AND THE DRAGON

George "The Animal" Steele and Ricky "The Dragon" Steamboat formed one of the most entertaining partnerships ever seen in WWE. The unlikely allies had a common enemy in Randy "Macho Man" Savage. Steele celebrating with The Dragon after his victory at *WrestleMania III* is

GOLDUST

When Goldust wears his platinum wig he appears even more enigmatic.

Goldust has used a variety of paint designs over the years, each a different distortion of his face.

As the son of WWE Hall of Famer, Dusty Rhodes, Goldust's apple did not just fall far from the tree—it landed light years away in a bizarre world of perversion. Blanketed from head to toe in form-fitting black and gold latex, he conceals his face with matching paint. Goldust resembles a life size Academy Award for Weirdest Performer. When he first emerged, his seductive tone of voice and peculiar methods of pushing social norms unnerved and infuriated his rivals. Whether a "sick freak" or just a misunderstood oddball, Goldust was ahead of his time. His scandalous exploits became a cure for the common show before WWE's Attitude Era began. Twenty years later, The Bizarre One is still going strong in all his glittery glory. Perhaps in his warped mind, that was the plan all along. One thing is for sure, long after his final Curtain Call, everyone will remember the name, Goldust.

Goldust has several glistening robes to match his ring gear.

HEIGHT: 6 feet, 6 inches (198 cm)

WEIGHT: 232 pounds (105 kg)

HOMETOWN: Hollywood, CA

SIGNATURE MOVES: Curtain Call

HOMEFIELD ADVANTAGE?

Goldust once battled "Rowdy" Roddy Piper in the land of glitz, glamour, and red carpets. However, Piper got the last laugh in the infamous Hollywood Backlot Brawl at *WrestleMania XII*. Though Goldust lost in humiliating fashion, the revolutionary match remains a timeless moment in WWE history.

GORILLA MONSOON

Gorilla Monsoon was a giant in all aspects of sports-entertainment. One of WWE's most beloved figures, Monsoon called the action for an entire generation of WWE fans, including the first six *WrestleMania* events. His poignant calls helped stamp some of history's biggest moments into memory. He exclaimed, "Superfly perched fifteen feet high!" while Jimmy Snuka leaped to immortality. Later, he put Hulk Hogan and Andre the Giant's epic showdown in the proper perspective, stating, "The irresistible force meeting the immovable object!" Prior to commentating, Monsoon was a feared competitor. The nickname "Gorilla" was appropriate for his size. He mauled opponents with incredible strength. Even Muhammad Ali was no match in a WWE setting. When the boxing deity entered Gorilla's domain, he received an Airplane Spin for his troubles. Monsoon is one of WWE's foremost legends. A WWE original since 1963, his impact on both sides of the camera was immeasurable.

Monsoon was respected for his brainpower as a sports-entertainment visionary. If Mr. McMahon had not stepped up to purchase WWE from his father, Superstars may have reported to Mr. Monsoon's office on the top floor of the WWE Tower.

HEIGHT: 6 feet, 7 inches (201 cm)

WEIGHT: 401 pounds (182 kg)

HOMETOWN: Manchuria

SIGNATURE MOVE: Airplane Spin

POSITIONS HELD: Commentator, WWE President

BEHIND THE CURTAIN

Gorilla Monsoon's career spanned several decades. Toward the end, he played a key role backstage, where he is now immortalized at every WWE event. A sign reading "GORILLA" indicates the area where Superstars congregate right before hitting the stage.

GREAT KHALI

Khali once had a memorable stare down with the 4' 5" Hornswoggle. Later on, the two became unlikely allies from opposite ends of the proportional spectrum.

If you were to stand on Great Khali's shoulders, you could probably see all the way to his home country of India. Khali is a national hero in his home land and an A-lister in the Bollywood film scene. His larger-than-life presence has also made him an attraction on American silver screens and in the WWE ring. Since first arriving in 2006 he has towered above the entire WWE roster like a menacing spire. One of the only Superstars in history capable of looking Big Show in the eye, Khali has held his own in several titanic clashes with all of WWE's resident behemoths. It's a good thing this goliath has a sense of humor. Just stay on his good side and The Punjabi Giant is content to bust a move and charm the ladies. Set him on the warpath, and you are in for a world of hurt.

HEIGHT: 7 feet, 1 inch (216 cm)

WEIGHT: 347 pounds (157 kg)

HOMETOWN:
Dhirana, India

SIGNATURE MOVES:
Punjabi Plunge, Khali Vise Grip

Khali steps over the top rope as if stepping over a crack in the sidewalk.

PUNJABI CHAMP

In 2007, Khali entered a 20-man Battle Royal with the vacant World Heavyweight Championship up for grabs. After seventeen other competitors were eliminated, The Punjabi Giant was too much for Batista and The Big Red Monster Kane. Khali powered his two rivals over the top rope to become the first Indian-born World Champ.

GREG "THE HAMMER" VALENTINE

Greg Valentine's platinum hair was his most unmistakable feature for his entire career, but as part of Rhythm & Blues he dyed it black for solidarity.

Greg "The Hammer" Valentine's career in WWE touched three decades. Multiple generations still feel the brunt of his painful offense years after his retirement. Valentine partnered with Ric Flair in the 1970s. His Figure-Four Leg Lock was just as devastating as the Nature Boy's. He used the feared submission move and other forceful maneuvers to earn a reputation as a tough-as-nails competitor. Valentine is a second-generation Superstar. He followed in his father's footsteps, scuffling from territory to territory before signing with WWE. Valentine competed in the first five *WrestleManias*, and is one of the most celebrated Intercontinental Champions of the 1980s. At one point, no one was tough enough to take the title off his waist for nine months. He also gave WWE Champions such as Hulk Hogan and Bob Backlund all that they could handle. Whether swinging for singles or tag team hardware, no one hit harder than "The Hammer."

His last name and his heart-decked robe are synonymous with romance, but Valentine was anything but sweet in the ring.

HEIGHT: 6 feet (183 cm)

WEIGHT: 243 pounds (110 kg)

HOMETOWN: Seattle, WA

SIGNATURE MOVE:
Figure-Four Leglock

COMBINED STRENGTH

Greg Valentine's physical style made him a sought after partner throughout his career. He was part of two memorable tag teams in the 1980s. He paired with Brutus "The Barber" Beefcake in The Dream Team. Later on, he formed a headline act called Rhythm & Blues with Honky Tonk Man.

HACKSAW JIM DUGGAN

Duggan rarely swung his 2x4 in aggression, but his favorite foreign object always loomed as a deterrent to foul play.

Before Daniel Bryan, Hacksaw made beards cool in WWE.

"Hacksaw" Jim Duggan is a former football standout who took his three point stance from the gridiron to sports-entertainment. Brawny, boisterous, and American as the bald eagle, Duggan put together a long career that earned him a Hall of Fame ring in 2011. Hacksaw arrived in WWE during its boom period in the late 1980s. His colorful persona stood out even among his larger-than-life peers. With his trusty 2x4 in one hand and Old Glory in the other, Duggan defended the honor of the Stars and Stripes against some of history's most notorious foreign villains. At *WrestleMania III*, over 93,000 fans rejoiced when he cleared the ring of the detested Iron Sheik and Nikolai Volkoff. Hacksaw still inspires chants of "USA! USA!" whenever he turns up in WWE. This happy-go-lucky fan favorite still stays in great shape just in case any "tough guys" get any ideas about messing with his beloved homeland.

Hacksaw often returned the fans' support with a cheerful "thumbs up" gesture to the crowd.

HEIGHT: 6 feet, 3 inches (191 cm)

WEIGHT: 270 pounds (122 kg)

HOMETOWN: Glens Falls, NY

SIGNATURE MOVE:
Three Point Stance Clothesline

RUMBLE HISTORY

The Royal Rumble is one of the most time-honored traditions in WWE. Just twenty-two competitors in history can claim victory in the over-the-top-rop melee. Only Jim Duggan, however, can say he was the first. Hacksaw won t inaugural Royal Rumble in 1988, earning a permanent place in history.

HARLEY RACE

Harley Race was a cerebral competitor in more ways than one. He was a perennial student of the game, constantly honing his skills. He also used his ruffled dome to level opponents for a three-count.

Harley Race was already sports-entertainment royalty long before he graced a WWE ring. It is only fitting that WWE fans knew him as "King" Harley Race. The Hall of Famer spent much of the 1970s and early '80s defending the NWA's World Heavyweight Championship against the likes of Ric Flair, Dusty Rhodes, and Terry Funk. When he arrived in WWE, he continued his dominance, winning the 1986 King of the Ring tournament. In his only *WrestleMania* match, Race defeated Junkyard Dog. Though JYD refused to kiss his feet, Race proved he could rule on the grandest stage. Wherever he competed, Harley's bone-tough aggression left a lasting impact. Tales of his toughness are told with reverence by all who felt the brunt of his smash-mouth style. Race's work ethic was peerless. For his tireless commitment to his craft, career longevity, and sheer dominance, Race was the epitome of the word "champion."

After a car accident early in his career, doctors told Harley Race he might never walk again and nearly amputated his leg. After months of excruciating therapy, Race made a full recovery and competed for almost thirty more years.

HEIGHT: 6 feet, 1 inch (185 cm)

WEIGHT: 253 pounds (115 kg)

HOMETOWN: Kansas City, MO

SIGNATURE MOVE:
Fisherman Suplex,
Diving Headbutt, Piledriver

RACE AT RINGSIDE

Taking advice from Harley Race proved to be a sound strategy for WCW stars Lex Luger and Vader. After the sun set on his in-ring career, Race became a manager and led both of these stars to notable reigns as WCW Champion.

HEATH SLATER

Heath Slater's flame colored hair stands out in a crowd, though he has yet to borrow spiking gel from Sheamus.

Heath Slater's motor mouth tends to get him into trouble. Perhaps that is why he has traveled as part of a pack for most of his career. The cocky Superstar has been a foot soldier in the renegade Nexus, an equal member of The Corre's round table, and the fiery-haired front man for the musical misfits known as 3MB. Now, the man who first dubbed himself a "One Man Band" is determined to once again forge ahead on his own and start backing up his words. Though his last solo act found him on the short end of several encounters with WWE's legends, Slater believes he has yet to hit his stride in WWE. He has tasted success before. Having won the Tag Team Titles with Justin Gabriel, Slater knows his potential. Once this young athlete gains momentum, his detractors may be forced to start singing a different tune.

Slater's outfits have varied over the years, particularly with 3MB. The trio produced historical and geographical inspired looks such as The Union Jacks, Rhinestone Cowboys, Fabulous 3Birds, and Plymouth Rockers.

HEIGHT: 6 feet, 2 inches (188 cm)

WEIGHT: 216 pounds (98 kg)

HOMETOWN: Pineville, WV

NOT FEELING THE FLO?

Heath Slater and hip-hop star Flo Rida have a grudge dating back to *WrestleMania XXVIII* in Miami. Two years after their infamous backstage confrontation, Flo Rida once again shoved Slater to the ground on *Raw*. The music star has not had a match with Slater, however, where the result would likely be much different.

HIDEO ITAMI

When the immortal Hulk Hogan presides over a ceremonial contract signing, you know it must be a big deal. Such was the case when the Hulkster landed in Osaka, Japan, to officially usher in the era of Hideo Itami in NXT. Renowned throughout the world by his former ring name, KENTA, Hideo is one of the most accomplished competitors in the history of Japan, a nation rich in sports-entertainment tradition. His humble manner may tell you otherwise, but Hideo has the firepower in the ring to handle opponents of all shapes and sizes. Described as a dynamic high flyer with a vicious streak, Hideo racked up a treasure trove of championships and accolades in his homeland. Now, with a new name dedicated to one of his heroes, he plans to replicate this success on the big stage, but first he must prove himself all over again on NXT. Hideo welcomes the challenge.

HEIGHT: 5 feet, 9 inches (175 cm)

WEIGHT: 182 pounds (83 kg)

HOMETOWN: Tokyo, Japan

Daniel Bryan has great respect for Hideo's abilities dating back to several clashes on the independent scene. Bryan even credits one of Hideo's many maneuvers as being the inspiration for his Running Knee that has helped propel him to the WWE World Heavyweight Championship.

Seth Rollins speaks from experience about competing against Hideo. Says Rollins about his lethal skill set, "That guy kicks harder than any human being I've ever seen in my life, and I don't know how anyone is getting up."

AN UNWELCOMING COMMITTEE
Hideo Itami's arrival in NXT was met with pageantry and celebration. The Ascension, however, did not share the warm feelings. One of NXT's most dominant entities, the sinister duo targeted Hideo repeatedly during his first few weeks in NXT. Hideo stood up to the attacks, sending a message that he will not be intimidated.

HILLBILLY JIM

Hillbilly Jim boasted one of the bushiest beards in all of WWE.

Don't go messin' with a country boy, especially if that country boy is Hillbilly Jim. First seen by the WWE Universe as an eager Hulkamaniac, Hillbilly was given his first pair of wrestling boots by the Hulkster himself, the ultimate endorsement. Looking to make his hero proud, the well-fed mountain man earned his boots by throwing down with WWE's most dangerous foes. He may have seemed like an affable, knee-slapping farmhand on the surface, but his towering size and powerful offensive moves made him a legitimate force in WWE. In front of over 93,000 fans at *Wrestlemania III*, Hillbilly Jim stood up to the menacing King Kong Bundy. The way he rushed to the aid of the pint-sized Little Beaver showed fans why Hillbilly was a friend they could trust. Years later, an old fashioned hootenanny still breaks out whenever Hillbilly Jim's catchy theme song is heard. Fans clap along with delight for this beloved legend.

His horseshoe necklace was a bit unorthodox, but Hillbilly was a perfect fit for WWE.

Though dressed for wallowing in pig slop, Hillbilly Jim proved that overalls could be effective ring attire.

HEIGHT: 6 feet, 7 inches (201 cm)
WEIGHT: 320 pounds (145 kg)
HOMETOWN: Mudlick, KY
SIGNATURE MOVE: Bear Hug

FAMILY MATTERS
Hillbilly Jim did not hog the sports-entertainment trait in the family gene pool. He routinely teamed up with his Uncle Elmer and his cousins, Luke and Junior. Years later, he mentored two more cousins, Henry and Phineas Godwinn, as they carried on the family tradition in WWE.

HONKY TONK MAN

With his long side burns and hair slicked back, he's going to hit your town in his pink Cadillac.

From the flared collar to the blue suede shoes, Honky Tonk Man was dressed to deliver a hunka hunka Honky love.

He's cool, he's cocky, and he's bad. He is the Honky Tonk Man. This guitar-wielding crooner strolled into WWE in 1986. Looking like he was plucked right off the Las Vegas strip, Honky Tonk Man seemed to fancy himself a contemporary King of Rock & Roll. WWE crowds disagreed. Despite the slicked black hair and gaudy polyester, his performances were not met with cries for an encore. The cascade of boos would have most people singing the blues, but Honky Tonk Man kept right on with the show. The louder they jeered, the harder he would shake, rattle and roll. This unflappable mindset and, of course, some well-timed swings of his trusty instrument carried him to great success. He kept a stranglehold on the Intercontinental Championship for 454 days, the longest reign in history. Honky Tonk Man has long since left the building, but his rhythm and style left a lasting mark in WWE.

Aside from carrying a tune, Honky Tonk Man used his six-string for other purposes. He once used it to plant Jake "The Snake" Roberts with a fierce blow to the noggin.

HEIGHT: 6 feet, 1 inch (185 cm)

WEIGHT: 243 pounds (110 kg)

HOMETOWN: Memphis, TN

SIGNATURE MOVE: Shake, Rattle and Roll

AN ABRUPT FINALE

"Give me someone out here to wrestle. I don't care who it is." Honky Tonk Man soon regretted those bold words when Ultimate Warrior came charging down the aisle at *SummerSlam 1988*. The open challenge backfired. Warrior pinned Honky Tonk in under a minute to end his historic title reign. The loss was bitter, but Honky Tonk Man still helped create a timeless moment in history.

HORNSWOGGLE

Communication was a challenge for Hornswoggle until a *Christmas* miracle gave him the ability to speak.

HEIGHT:
4 feet, 5 inches (135 cm)

WEIGHT:
142 pounds (64 kg)

SIGNATURE MOVES:
Tadpole Splash

Hornswoggle is living proof that big things do indeed come in small packages. Throughout history, hundreds of Superstars have battled for supremacy above the ring. Under the ring, however, is no contest. Hornswoggle has proven more lethal than any foreign object lurking behind the ring skirts from which he emerged in 2006. Though he barely approaches the waist of your typical WWE Superstar, Hornswoggle has produced a mountain of mischief. Expect the unexpected from this tiny terrorizer. He has done it all, from competing in the *Royal Rumble*, to rocking out with 3MB and breaking it down with DX. One bizarre incident even led the Chairman himself to believe he had fathered a mini-McMahon. While Hornswoggle's heredity is still not 100% clear, one thing is. No one is safe from his zany carnival of controversy. The look in his eyes spells mayhem, and only he knows what he is plotting.

Hornswoggle can grow a better beard than most men three times his size.

He may not live at the end of a rainbow but his affinity for green is one trait he does share with leprechauns of folklore.

YOU'VE GOT MAIL

For over a year, *Raw* was ruled from a laptop computer at ringside. Communicating only with Michael Cole via email, the anonymous *Raw* General Manager confounded the WWE roster. His whimsical decision making and whacky stipulations left many wondering what kind of whacko had been left in charge. Like most good mysteries, the answer was obvious. It had been Hornswoggle all along.

HOWARD FINKEL

He boasts one of the most amazing *WrestleMania* streaks in WWE history, spanning decades on the Grandest Stage of Them All. Undertaker? Nope, we are talking about Howard Finkel. Howard likes to jest that he is 30-0 at the Show of Shows, being the only personality to appear at each event. All joking aside, his resounding voice has ushered in the championship reigns of WWE's greatest icons: Hulk Hogan, Ultimate Warrior, Bret Hart, Stone Cold Steve Austin, and many more. Today, Howard serves as WWE's most long-standing employee. He shares his unrivaled historical knowledge on the pages of wwe.com and reminisces with fellow Legends for the WWE Universe to enjoy. When he steps into the ring, it is like a rare treat, taking fans on a trip down memory lane to the glory days of Madison Square Garden. In 2009, Howard became a deserving...NEEEWWWWW member of the WWE Hall of Fame.

Rare attempts at competing have resulted in Howard losing his tuxedo, revealing his red BVDs for the world to see. Fans cannot forget this memorable image, as hard as they might try.

HOMETOWN: Stamford, CT

FINKUS MAXIMUS

The WWE Universe is accustomed to seeing "The Fink" dressed to the nines in his finest tuxedos. At *WrestleMania IX*, however, Howard embraced the theme for the evening. Clothed in Roman Empire regalia, "Finkus Maximus" made his one and only appearance in a WWE ring.

HULK HOGAN

"Whatcha gonna do when Hulkamania runs wild on you?" For 30 years, no one has found the answer to this legendary query. Hulk Hogan became an American hero when he toppled the reviled Iron Sheik for the WWE Championship. Since then, no one has personified WWE more than the man in red and yellow. When WWE became a mainstream sensation in the 1980s, Hogan was at the forefront, flexing his 24-inch pythons. He teamed with Mr. T in the first *WrestleMania* main event, slammed Andre the Giant in front of 93,173 fans, and inspired an entire generation to "say their prayers and eat their vitamins."

When Hogan rips off his iconic red and yellow t-shirt, he is ready for action.

The Hulkster whips the crowd into frenzy just by cupping a hand to his ear.

HEIGHT:
6 feet, 7 inches (201 cm)

WEIGHT: 302 pounds (137 kg)

HOMETOWN: Venice Beach, CA

SIGNATURE MOVE:
Big Boot, Leg Drop

The Big Boot flattens opponents, setting them up for a thunderous Leg Drop.

The Hulkster was the only worthy host for WWE's milestone 30th *WrestleMania*. Now he is back where it all began and you can bet that Hulkamania will live forever, brother!

N.W.O

Hulk Hogan once reinvented himself by joining the renegade faction, n.W.o. Decked in black and white, "Hollywood" Hulk Hogan revealed his dark side, committing heinous acts with cohorts Hall and Nash. Eventually, nostalgia proved too powerful and Hulk returned to his roots as a Real American.

IRON SHEIK

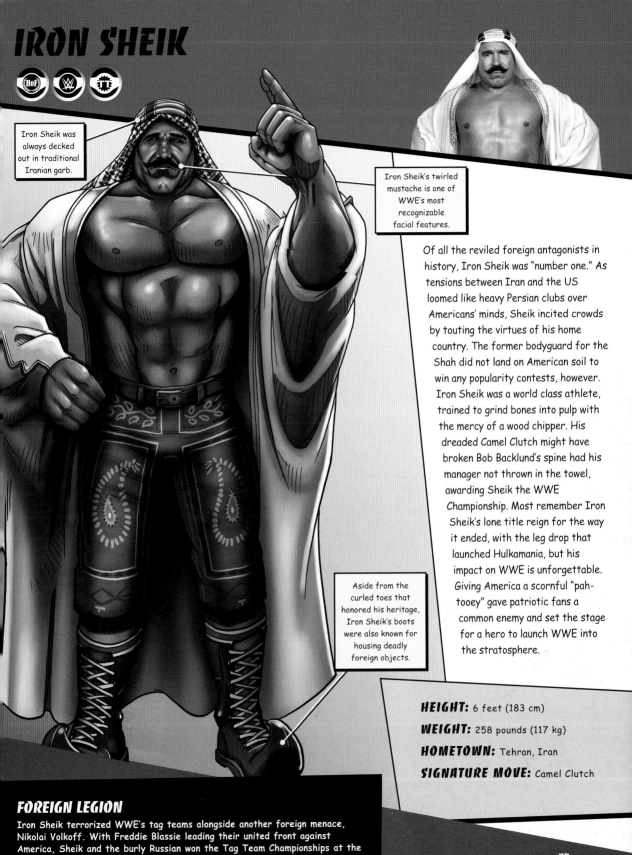

Iron Sheik was always decked out in traditional Iranian garb.

Iron Sheik's twirled mustache is one of WWE's most recognizable facial features.

Of all the reviled foreign antagonists in history, Iron Sheik was "number one." As tensions between Iran and the US loomed like heavy Persian clubs over Americans' minds, Sheik incited crowds by touting the virtues of his home country. The former bodyguard for the Shah did not land on American soil to win any popularity contests, however. Iron Sheik was a world class athlete, trained to grind bones into pulp with the mercy of a wood chipper. His dreaded Camel Clutch might have broken Bob Backlund's spine had his manager not thrown in the towel, awarding Sheik the WWE Championship. Most remember Iron Sheik's lone title reign for the way it ended, with the leg drop that launched Hulkamania, but his impact on WWE is unforgettable. Giving America a scornful "pah-tooey" gave patriotic fans a common enemy and set the stage for a hero to launch WWE into the stratosphere.

Aside from the curled toes that honored his heritage, Iron Sheik's boots were also known for housing deadly foreign objects.

HEIGHT: 6 feet (183 cm)

WEIGHT: 258 pounds (117 kg)

HOMETOWN: Tehran, Iran

SIGNATURE MOVE: Camel Clutch

FOREIGN LEGION

Iron Sheik terrorized WWE's tag teams alongside another foreign menace, Nikolai Volkoff. With Freddie Blassie leading their united front against America, Sheik and the burly Russian won the Tag Team Championships at the first *WrestleMania*.

IRWIN R. SCHYSTER

IRS wears these specs while taking a thorough look at your federal tax forms.

You would buy these same suspenders and tie combo if only you were in a higher tax bracket.

In the early '90s, tax cheats answered to one man, Irwin R. Schyster. The cold-hearted Superstar came to WWE armed with a calculator and skillful wrestling acumen. IRS was determined to wallop all of his rivals in the two places it hurt most, the ring and the bank account. Taxes are one of life's rare guarantees, and he was out to seize every last penny one way or another. IRS was most dominant as part of a joint venture with another financially savvy Superstar, "Million Dollar Man" Ted DiBiase. Money Inc. banked some serious assets in the form of three Tag Team Championships. The two symbols of greed continued their association as part of The Million Dollar Corporation. IRS gained enforcers in King Kong Bundy and Bam Bam Bigelow. To this day, he is still on the prowl, looking for any discrepancies in your tax records and waiting to collect.

HEIGHT: 6 feet, 3 inches (191 cm)

WEIGHT: 248 pounds (112 kg)

HOMETOWN: Washington D.C.

SIGNATURE MOVE:
The Write-Off

DOWN PAYMENT

In 2007, IRS made a surprising return on the *Raw* 15th Anniversary episode. He appeared to have won a hard-fought battle royal until his old running mate DiBiase appeared. The Million Dollar Man paid Schyster to eliminate himself, ending the match. All these years later, IRS still had a price.

JACK SWAGGER

Jack Swagger was bred in America's heartland and swells with patriotic pride. Swagger is as American as fireworks on the Fourth of July, even if his views of what constitutes a "Real American" have been narrow at best. Since the xenophobic Zeb Colter convinced Swagger to drink his Kool-Aid, the accomplished amateur grappler has displayed a more aggressive side. Swagger's raw athletic tools have always stacked up against the best in the business. As confident as his surname would indicate, Swagger flaunts these tools like a Hollywood caricature of the college jock. He has stockpiled a lifetime's worth of athletic achievements and has no intention of stopping, even if it means aligning with the controversial Colter. Now that his dangerous side has been unleashed, he possesses one of WWE's deadliest submission holds. Get trapped in his signature Patriot Lock, and you'll be standing for the Pledge of Allegiance on one foot.

Swagger stays true to his amateur roots with his double strapped singlet.

Swagger leads his supporters in a chant of "We the people!" with a hand over his heart.

HEIGHT: 6 feet, 7 inches (201 cm)

WEIGHT: 260 pounds (118 kg)

HOMETOWN: Perry, OK

SIGNATURE MOVES: Patriot Lock

CHAMPIONSHIP CURRENCY

Swagger claimed the Money in the Bank briefcase at *WrestleMania XXVI* and wasted very little time in capitalizing on it, taking his briefcase to *SmackDown*. A brutal encounter between Edge and Chris Jericho gave him the chance he was looking for. He swooped in to pin a tired Y2J, proving that WWE, much like America, is a land of opportunity.

JAKE "THE SNAKE" ROBERTS

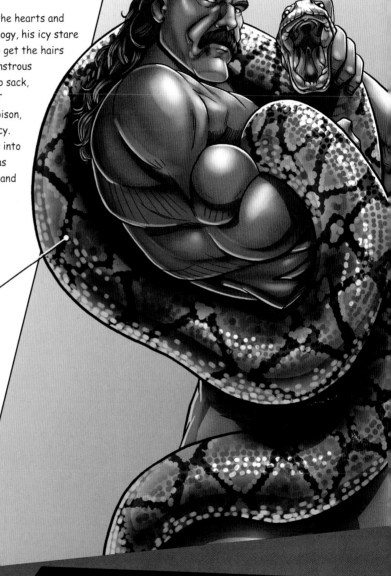

Jake "The Snake" Roberts instilled fear in the hearts and minds of his opponents. A master of psychology, his icy stare and ominous way of speaking were enough to get the hairs on one's arms standing at attention. The monstrous Damien, a python lying in wait within a burlap sack, added to the terror. Roberts' patented DDT finishing move, named after a type of rat poison, finished off opponents with deadly efficiency. This serpentine Superstar slithered his way into the history books, clashing with icons such as Randy Savage, Ricky Steamboat, Rick Rude, and others before retiring from WWE. He now holds a deserved spot in the WWE Hall of Fame, assuring his legacy will last forever, along with our nightmares.

Damien accompanied Jake until Earthquake crushed him beneath his massive frame, provoking Jake to unleash Lucifer, Damien's older brother.

HEIGHT: 6 feet, 6 inches (198 cm)

WEIGHT: 249 pounds (113 kg)

HOMETOWN: Stone Mountain, GA

SIGNATURE MOVE: DDT

WEDDING CRASHER

Jake Roberts ruined the wedding celebration of Randy Savage and Miss Elizabeth by unleashing a king cobra on the happy couple. In one of the most horrific sights in WWE history, the ravenous snake sank its fangs into Savage's arm, drawing blood.

JASON ALBERT

As Tensai, his head bore an even strip of Japanese lettering, but the temporary tattoo has been removed for his desk job.

Albert was always known for his piercings and still has enough to set off an airport metal detector.

Jason Albert's in-ring career spans multiple eras and continents. Today, this mysterious Superstar brings his well-rounded viewpoints to WWE's dynamic broadcast team. Working mostly on NXT and pay-per-view panels, he provides insight that can only come from years of competing around the globe reinventing one's personality. WWE fans first glimpsed this walking locomotive during the Attitude Era. Going by Albert and later A-Train, he derailed some of the toughest competition in WWE and even attempted to end Undertaker's Streak at *WrestleMania XIX*. Struggling to gain championship hardware, he crossed the Pacific to Japan. When he reemerged as Tensai, he displayed a more punishing arsenal and even though he discovered his sweet side shortly after, was still as imposing as ever. No matter how you remember his career as an active competitor, you can be sure he will charge into broadcasting with the same focused tenacity.

HEIGHT: 6 feet, 7 inches (201 cm)

WEIGHT: 360 pounds (163 kg)

HOMETOWN: Boston, MA

FAR EAST FEROCITY

When Tensai returned from his sojourn to Japan, his American lineage seemed like a distant memory. With a new manager, Sakamoto, he unveiled a Clawhold and even spit green mist. Unfortunately for his companion, he never learned to channel his fury. Mired in a losing streak, he brutally attacked Sakamoto and set off alone, in a land that now seemed foreign.

JASON JORDAN

Jason Jordan has a long list of options when deciding where to focus his energy. As a young athlete, Jordan excelled in football, baseball, and wrestling. He is no dummy either. Not only does this multi-talented NXT star have a degree in biology, he minored in chemistry, medicine, and social science. Jordan could have gone to school to become a dentist. However, when you boast a 35-0 record in the Big Ten's 285 pound wrestling weight class, and you only weigh 225 pounds, the allure of a WWE career is too enticing to pass up. Now, Jason is chasing his dream as part of the NXT roster, where his can-do attitude has turned heads in his young career. Jason Jordan is used to being a winner. He plans to settle for nothing less than the NXT Championship on his way to a long and successful career competing for WWE gold.

Jason Jordan has his initials, double J, etched on his gear.

HEIGHT: 6 feet, 3 inches (191 cm)

WEIGHT: 245 pounds (111 kg)

HOMETOWN: Chicago, IL

SIGNATURE MOVE: Jordan Slam

NAME THAT TAG TEAM

Jason Jordan paired up with another promising star, Tye Dillinger, in 2014. While they struggled to find a name for their team, at one point asking the WWE Universe for help, they did not struggle for chemistry. The duo formed a dynamic combo and competed with the best teams in NXT.

JBL

JBL polishes up for the boardroom but still owns several cowboy hats.

JBL is a titan among bulls and bears, whether he is standing in a WWE ring or on Wall Street. A self-made millionaire, JBL could have lived the good life on business acumen alone, raking in the dough from behind a solid oak desk in a cozy, corner office. But the allure of a fight is too much for the tough tycoon to resist. You can take the brawler out of Texas, but this relocated roughneck is always ready for a fight. Just ask the multitude of big name Superstars who failed to defeat him for the WWE Championship for nearly a year, or the unfortunate bartenders tasked with cleaning the carnage from Bradshaw and fellow APA bruiser Ron Simmons. With nothing left to prove in active competition, JBL gives his no-holds-barred account of the action each week on *Raw* and *SmackDown*, often getting a laugh at Michael Cole's expense.

JBL wears a three-piece suit these days but still keeps his windbreaker and black ring trunks in his limo in case they're needed.

HEIGHT: 6 feet, 6 inches (198 cm)

WEIGHT: 290 pounds (132 kg)

HOMETOWN:
New York, NY

SIGNATURE MOVES:
Clothesline from Hell

BAR ROOM BRAWLERS

JBL competed in several tag teams, but his most infamous pairing was with Ron Simmons, aka Faarooq. Together, the beer swilling, card playing, cigar-smoking ruffians were the best protection money could buy during the Attitude Era.

99

JERRY "THE KING" LAWLER

Lawler's crown is the hallmark of his royal regalia.

Jerry Lawler often drives his fist down on his opponent from the second rope.

HEIGHT:
6 feet (183 cm)

WEIGHT:
243 pounds (110 kg)

HOMETOWN:
Memphis, TN

SIGNATURE MOVE:
Piledriver

Jerry "The King" Lawler has the best seat in the house for all the non-stop action in WWE. As WWE's lead color commentator, The King has ruled the announce table for nearly twenty years. Alongside fellow Hall of Famer Jim Ross, he provided the vivacious soundtrack for WWE's bold Attitude Era. Today, he continues to entertain millions of viewers with his insatiable wit and endless supply of one-liners.

Today's fans know him for his lively analysis from ringside, but The King is royalty inside the ropes as well. When situations warrant, he is ready to hit the canvas and relive his early years as a wrestling legend. The Miz found this out in 2011 when Lawler nearly defeated him for the WWE Championship. Whether stockpiling championships in various territories, slapping comedians on late night TV, disparaging ECW, or ogling the WWE Divas, Jerry Lawler's fascinating career proves that it's good to be The King.

Clad in-ring gear under his announcing garb, Lawler is ready to compete (or assist one of the Divas) at a moment's notice.

KISS MY FEET

Lawler suffered his worst humiliation in 1995. Bret "Hit Man" Hart forced him to eat his words...and his stinking feet in a Kiss My Foot Match. Years later, he relived this moment on the favorable end when he served his royal toes to Michael Cole with a side of barbeque sauce.

JERRY SAGS

The Nasty Boys shaved their heads into twin mullets on opposite sides of the color spectrum. Sags wore his jet-black.

Jerry Sags had a nasty reputation by the time he and partner, Brian Knobbs, brought their sweaty, toothless snarl to WWE in the early 1990s. Having already bashed heads with the hardest hitting tag teams in various stops this side of Nastyville, the Nasty Boys promised to inflict the same brand of aggression on WWE. With Jimmy Hart's encouraging words echoing through his trusty megaphone, the notorious troublemakers clashed with The Road Warriors, Hart Foundation and several other top teams. It was never pretty, but the Nasties could care less for style points. Sags put the finishing touches on the team's "nastycized" opponents, landing a vicious diving elbow. Their stay in WWE was short, but memorable. In just over two years, they clobbered their way to a noteworthy Tag Team Title reign and turned boos from the WWE Universe into cheers. Who says Sags has a face only a mother could love?

The Nasty Boys were rarely seen without their black shades.

When their matches began, Sags and Knobbs ditched their black trench coats to reveal their flashy, neon ring attire.

HEIGHT: 6 foot, 3 inches (191 cm)

WEIGHT: 290 pounds (132 kg)

HOMETOWN: Allentown, PA

SIGNATURE MOVES: Pit Stop, Trip to Nastyville

NOW THAT'S NASTY

Before Rikishi unleashed his Stinkface move in WWE, Sags and Knobbs grossed out their foes by introducing them face-first to the stench of their armpits. Sags, like their double-crossing manager Jimmy Hart, might

JEY USO

Jey's face paint mirrors his brother Jimmy's and embodies his desire to compete and thrive.

THE USOS

The Usos each have their share of ink. Jey began with a cross on his arm and now displays a full sleeve of tribal designs.

When he says "UUSS," you say "OOOH!!" Jey Uso descends from one of the most revered bloodlines in sports-entertainment history, the Samoan Anoa'i family. Along with his twin brother, Jimmy, Jey is a contemporary version of his island-born predecessors. Refusing to be typecast as barefoot competitors strewn with beads, The Usos wear customary boots and trunks in the ring. The brothers blend seamlessly with their American peers while keeping the celebrated essence of their ancestors alive in WWE. The Usos' passionate drive to compete and succeed was evident when they first emerged in WWE and still shows today. When rival tag teams see this face-painted pair up on the entrance ramp performing the Siva Tau, they know they are in for a long night. Jey and Jimmy are determined to take their proud lineage into the 21st century and leave their own lasting legacy in WWE.

HEIGHT: 6 feet, 2 inches (188 cm)

WEIGHT: 228 pounds (103 kg)

HOMETOWN: San Francisco, CA

FAMILY TREE

If heritage is any indication, The Usos will bring a surge of excitement to WWE for years to come. Along with their father, the legendary Rikishi, members of their illustrious family include WWE Hall of Famers The Wild Samaons and "The Most Electrifying Man in All of Entertainment," The Rock.

JIM ROSS

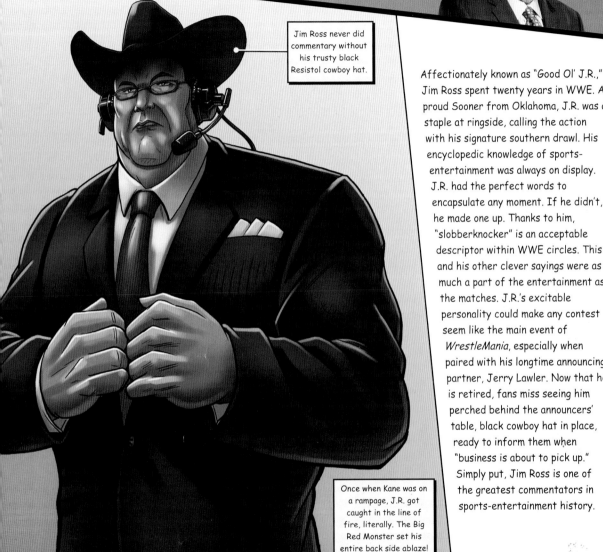

Jim Ross never did commentary without his trusty black Resistol cowboy hat.

Once when Kane was on a rampage, J.R. got caught in the line of fire, literally. The Big Red Monster set his entire back side ablaze!

Affectionately known as "Good Ol' J.R.," Jim Ross spent twenty years in WWE. A proud Sooner from Oklahoma, J.R. was a staple at ringside, calling the action with his signature southern drawl. His encyclopedic knowledge of sports-entertainment was always on display. J.R. had the perfect words to encapsulate any moment. If he didn't, he made one up. Thanks to him, "slobberknocker" is an acceptable descriptor within WWE circles. This and his other clever sayings were as much a part of the entertainment as the matches. J.R.'s excitable personality could make any contest seem like the main event of *WrestleMania*, especially when paired with his longtime announcing partner, Jerry Lawler. Now that he is retired, fans miss seeing him perched behind the announcers' table, black cowboy hat in place, ready to inform them when "business is about to pick up." Simply put, Jim Ross is one of the greatest commentators in sports-entertainment history.

HOMETOWN: Westville, OK

BAH GAWD!!
J.R. preferred to let the athletes handle the physicality, but found himself needing to knuckle up on occasion. He taught his successor, Michael Cole, a lesson with a "country whippin'." He also has a win over Triple H in the record books, though Batista did all the heavy lifting.

JIMMY HART

Due to Jimmy Hart's underhanded tactics, the megaphone has won more matches than some Superstars.

"The Mouth of the South" Jimmy Hart is a Hall of Fame manager who was never short on words or clients. Hart steered the course of several prestigious careers from his namesakes in the Hart Foundation to the Nasty Boys, Rhythm and Blues, and numerous others. Like all managers, his natural speaking ability made his clients sound like a million bucks. But one unique tool allowed his message to ring louder than his peers—the megaphone. Jimmy Hart's notorious device projected his voice all the way to the cheap seats. The loudhailer also had a way of being inserted into matches. Between his constant yapping at ringside and mischief behind the referee's back, Hart was reviled by opponents. Every so often, a fortunate protagonist would manage to get his hands on the mouthy troublemaker. Crowds would rejoice but he always reemerged, loud and proud, ready to shout to the hilltops.

Jimmy Hart's wardrobe was as colorful as his personality. His jackets were airbrushed with vibrant colors, themed for his clients. Because he had so many charges, he changed several times during events.

HEIGHT: 5 feet, 10 inches (178 cm)

HOMETOWN: Memphis, TN

SUPERSTARS MANAGED:
The Hart Foundation, Greg Valentine, Honky Tonk Man, The Natural Disasters, The Nasty Boys, The Mountie, The Mega Maniacs, Money Inc., Dino Bravo, The Fabulous Rougeau Brothers, Danny Davis, King Kong Bundy, and others.

AN IMMORTAL COMBINATION

Jimmy Hart spent the bulk of his lengthy career antagonizing crowds, but all was forgiven when he sided with the iconic Hulk Hogan. With the Hulkster and Brutus "The Barber" Beefcake in tow, fans excused his past transgressions. Their team, dubbed The Mega Maniacs, stood up to the greedy Ted DiBiase and other evildoers.

JIMMY "SUPERFLY" SNUKA

Snuka often curled his middle and ring fingers down to gesture an "I love you" to the crowd.

Snuka's skull withstood a coconut blast courtesy of Roddy Piper, but the Hot Rod's point blank fruiting remains one of WWE's most infamous incidents.

Jimmy Snuka did for WWE what the Wright brothers did for transportation. The island native proved that gravity was no excuse not to fly the friendly skies. Snuka's stratospheric assault not only propelled him to top flight status in WWE, it inspired an entire generation to think above the ropes. His most iconic leap was off a fifteen foot high Steel Cage at Madison Square Garden. A young Mick Foley witnessed it, as did several other Big Apple based youths with dreams of sports-entertainment glory. The majestic sight of Snuka soaring through the air served as their inspiration. His aerial advantage did not help him avoid becoming the first victim in Undertaker's *WrestleMania* Streak. Still, Superfly enjoyed an upper hand over many of his mat-based peers. Snuka transformed the top turnbuckle into a launching pad for WWE's more adventurous Superstars. Today, Superfly is perched in the WWE Hall of Fame.

Few high flyers in history would be worthy of lacing Snuka's boots, if he had worn any.

HEIGHT: 5 feet, 10 inches (178 cm)

WEIGHT: 235 pounds (107 kg)

HOMETOWN: The Fiji Islands

SIGNATURE MOVE: Superfly Splash

STILL AT CRUISING ALTITUDE

Jimmy Snuka supported Hulk Hogan and Mr. T from ringside at the first *WrestleMania*. Twenty-five years later, Superfly returned to the grandest stage to team with other Legends against Chris Jericho. The veteran impressed a whole new generation by showing off impressive athleticism for his age.

JIMMY USO

The Uso's matching war paint is symbolic of their determination to be WWE Tag Team Champions.

Jimmy Uso is one of the latest Superstars from the celebrated Anoa'i family to bring the glorious traditions of his ancestors to WWE. Ingrained in American culture with the spirit of the Samoan isle flowing through his veins, Jimmy brings the best of both worlds to the ring. He also brings an exact copy of himself in the form of his twin brother, Jey. In WWE's tag team division, no one can duplicate the natural chemistry of these identical siblings. Together, The Usos create a wild, up-tempo style that both delights the WWE Universe and wears down their rivals. They may not cut a rug quite like their dad, Rikishi, but the excitement they create each week makes this Legend a proud papa. Months before *WrestleMania 30*, Jimmy and Jey captured their first WWE Tag Team Championship. With warrior hearts and a rooted passion for success, this first taste of gold is only the beginning for this electrifying duo.

The Uso's trunks are decorated with the tribal imagery of the Pacific Islands.

THE USOS

HEIGHT: 6 feet, 3 inches (191 cm)

WEIGHT: 251 pounds (114 kg)

HOMETOWN: San Francisco, CA

SIVA TAU

All Superstars have their methods of getting psyched up for a match, but none like The Usos. The Siva Tau is an ancient Samoan war dance used to strike fear into the hearts of the enemy. Jimmy and Jey intimidate their opponents by performing this dance on the entrance ramp before heading into battle.

JOHN CENA

John Cena's symbolic victory over JBL at *WrestleMania 21* ushered in a changing of the guard in WWE. On that fateful night in Los Angeles a decade ago, Cena not only became "The Champ," he kick started his reign as the undeniable face of a generation. Since then, the Cenation leader has spent over 1300 days as a reigning World Champion and in June 2014 picked up title number fifteen! More importantly, he has redefined what being a champion means. His mantra of "Hustle, Loyalty and Respect" is more than just a catchy phrase. It is a way of life, and it reflects Cena's unwavering commitment. Like him or not, Cena will show up, give his absolute best and do the right thing. Cena's success is a result of this tireless work ethic. He is not done yet, by the way. Whenever he decides to hang up his sneakers, Cena's legacy might be unmatched.

John Cena's color coordinated assortment always makes a great souvenir for Cenation members sitting ringside.

Cena's often imitated "You Can't See Me" gesture has transcended WWE into mainstream pop culture, just like The Champ himself.

Rather than traditional tights and wrestling boots, Cena competes in a baggy pair of jean shorts and sneakers.

HEIGHT: 6 feet, 1 inch (185 cm)

WEIGHT: 251 pounds (114 kg)

HOMETOWN: West Newbury, MA

SIGNATURE MOVE: Attitude Adjustment, STF

FEATS OF STRENGTH

John Cena never misses a workout and is one of WWE's most powerful Superstars. At *WrestleMania 25* he hoisted both Edge and the 480-pound Big Show on his shoulders for an Attitude Adjustment.

JOHN LAURINAITIS

John Laurinaitis once presided over WWE's entire roster, calling the shots on *Raw* and *SmackDown* until Mr. McMahon told him WWE's two most dreaded words, "You're fired!" Big Johnny's dismissal and subsequent trip through the Spanish announcers' table delighted WWE fans. Laurinaitis preached a philosophy of "People Power," but the people saw through this thinly veiled propaganda. The smarmy executive had his own agenda and would use whatever resources necessary to fulfill it, from his smooth politician's grin to David Otunga's expensive legal counsel. His biggest power play came at *WrestleMania XXVIII* when his team upended Teddy Long's to earn him control of WWE's two flagship programs. He used knowledge from his in-ring career to become a shrewd negotiator behind the scenes and on camera. His ego may have been as inflated as his job title, but Johnny was still a certifiable big shot in WWE for several years.

Johnny did not appreciate having his raspy voice mocked. Soon after hearing Big Show's unflattering imitation, Laurinaitis gave The World's Largest Athlete his "future endeavors."

Laurinaitis was a corporate suit in WWE for several years and always looked the part.

WWE Superstars have poked fun at Big Johnny for being a skateboard enthusiast during his in-ring career.

HOMETOWN: Philadelphia, PA

POSITIONS HELD: Executive Vice President of Talent Relations, *Raw* General Manager, *SmackDown* General Manager

SECOND CITY SLIGHTS

John Laurinaitis was an unknown executive to most fans until CM Punk called him out in his famous "pipe bomb" rant. Calling him a "glad-handing, nonsensical Yes-man" (among other things) may have inspired Big Johnny to exert his authority on camera.

JUNKYARD DOG

Junkyard Dog endeared himself to fans of all walks of life. During WWE's golden age of expansion, JYD was one of the Superstars leading the charge. Adorned with his signature dog collar and chains, he did not just captivate the audience—he made them part of the show. JYD brought children into the ring to boogie down to the funky beats of "Grab Them Cakes," the hit entrance theme recorded by the Dog himself. In the ring, he proved to have a bite to match his bark. Junkyard Dog butted heads with WWE's most illustrious villains including Roddy Piper, "Cowboy" Bob Orton, and "King" Harley Race. Over 93,000 fans roared their approval when JYD refused to be bullied by the ruthless Race at *WrestleMania III*. His unique brand of showmanship has lived on through stars such as Rikishi, Brodus Clay, and others who inject WWE with their own dose of funk.

JYD's studded collar and chains added to his allure.

JYD preferred white or red tights with "THUMP" written on his backside.

HEIGHT:
6 feet, 3 inches (191 cm)

WEIGHT:
280 pounds (127 kg)

HOMETOWN:
Charlotte, NC

SIGNATURE MOVE:
"Thump" Powerslam

A TRUE CLASSIC

A common misconception is that *WrestleMania* was WWE's first pay-per-view. It was actually *The Wrestling Classic*, a 16-man King of the Ring-style tournament held months later. JYD defeated Randy Savage in the tournament final to become WWE's first winner in a pay-per-view main event, an amazing accolade that often gets lost in the annals of history.

JUSTIN GABRIEL

Justin Gabriel is a daring competitor with a flair for walking on the wild side. Whether by himself or with a pack of likeminded Superstars, Gabriel stands out from a crowd. He first showed off his high risk, 450 Splash as a member of both The Nexus and The Corre, proving to be dangerous on the mat and above the ropes. His pleasant smile might make him seem affable, but underestimating the South Africa native would be a mistake. Now a lone wolf, he remains as feisty as ever. When it comes to the rulebook, he has fallen on both sides of the fence and there is no telling where he will land next. His nasty side reveals itself at times to give him an edge but it is hard to dislike this charismatic Superstar. He thrilled fans on *NXT* Season 1 and now, for Gabriel, the future is here.

Justin Gabriel's long hair whips through the wind when he executes his 450 Splash.

Gabriel has recently been referred to as the Cape Town Dare-Wolf, and is furry like all lycanthropes of mythical folklore.

HEIGHT: 6 feet, 1 inch (185 cm)

WEIGHT: 213 pounds (97 kg)

HOMETOWN: Cape Town, South Africa

SIGNATURE MOVE: 450 Splash

JUMPING SHIP

Gabriel's 450 Splash often put a stamp on The Nexus's vicious attacks. However, when CM Punk assumed leadership of the black and yellow clan, Gabriel refused to take part in Punk's degrading initiation rituals. Gabriel and Heath Slater abandoned Nexus and joined The Corre.

JUSTIN ROBERTS

There is no "business casual" in-ring announcing. Roberts was always suited and clean shaven.

Justin Roberts grew up in the sports-entertainment hotbed of Chicago, Illinois. He went on to make a living doing what he practiced as a child on the playgrounds of the Second City. Justin has served as the ring announcer for WWE's flagship show, *Monday Night Raw*, and has joined Lilian Garcia and others to announce WWE's pay-per-view events. Justin has had the honor of welcoming the WWE Universe to *WrestleMania* in front of over 75,000 delirious fans. He has announced a main event match on the Grandest Stage featuring Undertaker and later, Brock Lesnar's breaking of The Streak. He has also been in the ring for the blockbuster returns of The Rock and Bret "Hit Man" Hart to WWE. Being tied to these historic moments is a fantasy for most fans. Justin Roberts is living proof that landing that dream job is only a matter of commitment and determination.

Holding a WWE mic is a privilege that Justin did not take lightly.

HEIGHT: 5 feet, 10 inches (178 cm)

WEIGHT: 170 pounds (77 kg)

HOMETOWN: Scottsdale, AZ

POSITIONS HELD:
Raw ring announcer,
SmackDown ring announcer

COLLATERAL DAMAGE

Justin Roberts' job was not always glamorous. When The Nexus made their notorious *Raw* debut, Roberts was caught in the crossfire of the rampaging renegades. The goons targeted John Cena and dismantled the *Raw* set, and Roberts took a pummeling in the process.

KALISTO

A luchador's mask is as important to his identity as his DNA. Kalisto takes pride in all his masks, which come in several different varieties and even feature spikes running down the middle.

Kalisto is known as the "King of Flight" and plans to take his lucha libre style to greater heights in WWE. Like all traditional luchadors, no one sees Kalisto's face. What fans do see are his innovative and mystifying combinations of moves performed at full throttle... provided fans don't blink. Kalisto's speed and agility make him one of the most exciting Superstars in NXT. He got WWE's attention by his spectacular displays of aerial artistry in the Mexican circuit. At this rate, it won't be long before Kalisto gets the whole world's attention. Kalisto is a hybrid Superstar. He derives his skill set from the eclectic styles of several others before him. With these combined strengths, it is impossible to predict what high flying moves he is plotting behind his mask. One thing is for certain, Kalisto has a "Wow" factor that leaves a lasting impact on all spectators.

HEIGHT: 5 feet, 6 inches (168 cm)

WEIGHT: 170 pounds (77 kg)

HOMETOWN: Mexico City, Mexico

MAS LUCHADORES!

Kalisto formed a team with another masked marvel, El Local, in 2014. The Mexican duo won their debut match against The Legionnaires and went on to compete in a hard fought rivalry with The Ascension for the NXT Tag Team Titles.

KAMALA

Kamala had a warrior's spirit which was reflected in his facial war paint and the tribal moons and stars on his chest.

Kamala could make the bravest explorers of the deep, dark African wilderness turn tail and run for their lives. Standing at a towering six-foot-seven (even with the absence of footwear), the menacing beast terrorized WWE. Wearing nothing but paint and a loincloth, the primitive Superstar proved impossible to control for all that tried. He did not speak a word of English, communicating only in savage grunts and slapping his sizable belly as if hungry for human brains. Kamala's faithful companion, Kim Chee, was more a handler than a manager. Even Chee could do little to tame the Ugandan Giant. Kamala never needed his rudimentary spear or shield in the ring. His towering size and petrifying appearance were enough to make life difficult for just about anyone courageous enough to face him. Kamala has long vanished from WWE. We can only assume he is now lurking in the dense jungle from which he emerged.

Kamala competed in the same loincloth that he wore in his primitive habitat.

HEIGHT: 6 feet, 7 inches (201 cm)

WEIGHT: 380 pounds (172 kg)

HOMETOWN: Uganda

SIGNATURE MOVE: Flying Splash

Of the many barefooted brawlers in history, Kamala is the largest to compete sans shoes.

DEADLY DISTINCTION

One Superstar who did not fear Kamala was Undertaker. An attempt by his handlers to sick Kamala on The Deadman led to the first ever Coffin Match. The untamed terrorizer gained the unfortunate distinction of being the first of many entombed by Undertaker.

KANE

THE RED MONSTER

Kane is the wicked embodiment of hellfire and brimstone in WWE. Plucked straight from your deepest, darkest childhood fears, The Devil's Favorite Demon has left a charred course of destruction in the ring for almost two decades. Behind his demonic mask, he unleashes his fiery fury on all who dare stoke his anger. His devilish deeds are too many to list. To do so would require enough paper to fuel a towering inferno, much like the one that left him burned as a child. Kane unleashed revenge on his half-brother Undertaker, whom he blames for the fire, on his WWE debut. Since then The Big Red Monster has been a twisted, disturbed version of his sinister sibling. Over the years he has unmasked, formed alliances, and even donned a corporate suit. Nevertheless, once a monster, always a monster. Make no mistake. Kane's fire still burns.

First used to conceal his burns, Kane's mask now symbolizes his infernal soul.

Kane keeps his Chokeslamming hand gloved for a better grip on his victims.

Kane's black ring attire could have been stitched in re[d] by Satan himself

HEIGHT: 7 feet (213 cm)

WEIGHT: 323 pounds (147 kg)

SIGNATURE MOVES:
Chokeslam

POSITIONS HELD:
WWE Director of Operations

OH BROTHER!

Kane and Undertaker have a long and sordid history. Together as The Brothers of Destruction, their blood bond makes them an indomitable force in the ring. That is, until old wounds open up, igniting their combustible rivalry.

KEVIN NASH

Kevin Nash is not a man you want to meet in a dark alley. Whether going by Diesel, his given name, or other monikers, his presence spells danger. Standing nearly seven feet tall and weighing over 300 pounds, "Big Daddy Cool" still finds opponents stuck to the bottom of his shoes to this day. Nash shook the foundation of sports-entertainment, smashed his way to the top, and loved himself for it. He may have been dubbed an "Outsider" at one point, but it was by his own design. A man Nash's size goes where he wants, when he wants. His most dangerous quality, however, is his mind. Nash orchestrated his path to success with cold, cunning efficiency. He was involved in perhaps the greatest coup in history, initiating a hostile takeover of WCW. He made enemies, caused trouble, pillaged the establishment, and walked away unscathed. You would have a massive ego too.

Kevin Nash's goatee made him look even more intimidating.

The logo on his tank top varied, from Diesel to n.W.o and others, but Nash always kept the same sleeveless style.

Nash was a blue-collar Superstar who competed in denim or leather pants.

HEIGHT: 6 feet, 10 inches (208 cm)

WEIGHT: 328 pounds (149 kg)

HOMETOWN: Detroit, MI

SIGNATURE MOVE:
Jackknife Powerbomb

ROYAL RETURN

A familiar horn erupted at the 2011 *Royal Rumble*. WWE fans recognized Diesel's entrance music instantly. Their excitement nearly blew the roof off! Diesel had spent several years away from WWE. For the next year he proved he was still a force in the ring, making life difficult for CM Punk and his ex-Kliq buddy Triple H.

KOFI KINGSTON

Kofi Kingston dazzles the WWE Universe with his boundless enthusiasm and mind boggling agility. Don't blink when Kofi is the ring. You might miss something amazing. This is especially true at WWE's *Royal Rumble*, where Kofi's virtuoso escape tactics have become as traditional as the event itself. The Boom Squad leader tops himself each year with his ingenious methods of staving off elimination. This creativity has been honed over an impressive career. Kofi has soared his way to multiple reigns with several prestigious titles, all with a beaming smile plastered on his face. His friendly persona and spirited style make Kofi one of the most popular Superstars in WWE. Still, he has his share of enemies and when tested, is quick to ratchet up the intensity and summon his inner "Wildcat." Whenever there is trouble in paradise, look to the skies for the Ghanaian Grappler leaping into action.

Don't let the friendly face fool you. Kofi is a fierce competitor.

Kofi's vertical leap gives him an edge against larger competitors.

HEIGHT: 6 foot (183 cm)

WEIGHT: 212 pounds (96 kg)

HOMETOWN: Ghana, West Africa

SIGNATURE MOVE: Trouble in Paradise

MADISON SQUARE GHANA

Kofi Kingston once defaced Randy Orton's prized stock car in a fit of rage. The Viper did not get the message. He continued to annoy Kingston in WWE's home, Madison Square Garden. As a result, the Dreadlock Dynamo performed a Boom Drop on Randy through a table.

KOKO B. WARE

Koko often wore expansive sunglasses, as if everywhere he went were a tropical paradise.

Koko B. Ware was a perfect fit for the colorful world of WWE. Though only 5' 7", Koko's multicolored outfits and infectious personality made him just as larger-than-life as his peers. His hyper energy and unquenchable thirst for competition earned him a passionate following. He enjoyed success as both a singles star and in a tag team appropriately named High Energy. However, Koko B. Ware's most well-known alliance was with his faithful pet macaw, Frankie. The winged companion added to "The Bird Man's" allure. Young fans were delighted to see the majestic bird and his master whenever they stepped through the curtain. "The Bird Man" never captured a championship in WWE, but he did not need one to win the hearts of the WWE Universe. That fact made Koko B. Ware a deserving member of the WWE Hall of Fame, an honor that he received (with Frankie by his side) in 2009.

Fans enjoyed flapping their wings along with "The Bird Man's" lovable mascot.

The only thing brighter than Koko B. Ware's outfits was the smile he wore each night he got to compete.

HEIGHT:
5 feet, 7 inches (170 cm)

WEIGHT: 228 pounds (103 kg)

HOMETOWN: Union City, TN

SIGNATURE MOVE:
Ghostbuster

SONG BIRD

WWE has a longstanding connection with its fans' love of music. Koko B. Ware shares some of this credit. In 1987, WWE produced its second music album. "The Bird Man" rocked as the lead vocals for "Piledriver," the album's hit single, and one of WWE's most illustrious music videos of all time.

117

KONNOR

In his frightening looking cloak, Konnor appears ready to cast a sea of minions into a pit of damnation.

If you are not yet freaked out by Konnor, you will be. This massive and menacing Superstar resembles a ruthless overlord from some unknown realm of the deep, dark underworld. With deep set eyes and an ominous presence, Konnor's stare can paralyze the weak-hearted with fear. The strong-hearted? They have a Full Nelson Slam or other devastating power display to look forward to. Konnor does not socialize with the NXT locker room. His lives his life in seclusion, communicating only with Viktor, his vicious partner in The Ascension. Having already laid claim to the NXT Tag Team Championship, no one knows for sure what Konnor's next move will be. He has the necessary power of both body and mind to wreak havoc on WWE. Konnor does not merely plan to conquer. He promises. In his words, "All will fail … and he will rise."

This all-seeing eye, seen on Konnor's ring gear, represents Ra, the Egyptian God of the sun and one of the most feared Gods in all of Egyptian mythology.

HEIGHT: 6 feet, 4 inches (193 cm)

WEIGHT: 265 pounds (120 kg)

HOMETOWN: Grand Rapids, MI

NXT CAREER HIGHLIGHTS:
NXT Tag Team Champion

ASCENDING TO GREATNESS

The Ascension began as a team of many but has forged ahead with only the two most worthy. Konnor and Viktor boast the longest ever reign with the NXT Tag Team Titles, keeping the prizes in their sinister clutches for just under a year.

LANA

Lana is the International Social Ambassador for Rusev, a menacing Superstar bent on "crushing" his opponents. Educated and well connected in the Russian socio-political landscape, Lana is planning a hostile takeover and has just the weapon to do it. Rusev operates on her command. His merciless power displays serve to spread her message that "Resistance is futile." Lana's boastful praise for the unpopular Russian leader, Vladimir Putin, has incited the WWE Universe, who can only watch while she revels in another vicious exhibition by her "super athlete." As Rusev continues to display his superiority, Lana becomes more aggressive in extolling his virtues. She seems to hold a domineering power over the Bulgarian Brute, and, like a bizarro-Lois Lane, has inspired his rampage against the American way. Lana's authoritative introductions of her client have bred anger and fear in the masses, and the Ravishing Russian has only begun.

Lana exudes both beauty and power in her executive attire.

HEIGHT:
5 feet, 7 inches (170 cm)

HOMETOWN:
Moscow, Russia

SUPERSTAR MANAGED: Rusev

"RUSEV, CRUSH"

Lana's forceful command of "Rusev, crush!" is like pushing the red button when the "super athlete" is in the ring. Once his demonstrations of speed and strength have reached her satisfaction, Rusev unleashes his finishing arsenal.

LAYLA

Layla is one of the most flawless Diva's Champions of all time. Beautiful, bubbly, and scrappy inside the ring, the British-born Diva has racked up a litany of accomplishments since dancing her way to WWE in 2006. Before LeBron arrived in South Beach, Layla took her talents to the Miami Heat dance squad and then the WWE Diva Search where she seized the once-in-a-lifetime opportunity, earning a WWE contract. She hasn't looked back since. She is part of an elite club of Divas to have held both the Diva's and Women's Championships, possessing the latter when the title was retired in 2010. She overtook her friend Michelle McCool as WWE's foremost mean girl, battled back from devastating injury to reclaim championship gold, and recently rediscovered her dancing shoes for a fleeting romance with the fancy-footed Fandango. Most WWE fans agree, Layla is one of the British Isle's greatest exports.

Layla's infinity symbol on her ring gear is worn as a tribute to her mother.

Whether in dancing shoes or ring boots, Layla is always ready to entertain.

HEIGHT: 5 feet, 3 inches (160 cm)

HOMETOWN: Miami, FL

SIGNATURE MOVES:
Infinity

LAY-COOL

Layla and Michelle McCool formed an alliance in 2010 based on a shared sense of vanity and arrogance. Calling themselves "flawless" the partners of perfection played mean-spirited pranks and hatched a scheme to be co-Women's Champions. The duo broke the Women's Title into two equal pieces so they could each carry half, infuriating Teddy Long.

LEX LUGER

It is amazing Lex Luger's arms were able to fit through the door of the Lex Express.

Lex Luger was "The Total Package," whether spreading patriotism up and down America's highways or running with the dominant Four Horsemen in WCW. The WWE Universe first saw him surrounded by mirrors, admiring his massive, tanned muscles from various angles. Luger soon got over himself, though, and focused on becoming an American hero. With his narcissistic ways behind him and the open road in front of him, he captained the flag-flying Lex Express. His greatest contribution to Americana was when he answered an open challenge from the menacing Japanese Superstar, Yokozuna. Aboard the USS Intrepid, Luger hoisted the quarter-ton giant and slammed him on the deck. His time in WWE was brief, but his impact was as massive as his biceps. Luger is also known for playing an instrumrntal role in the Monday Night War by making a shocking appearance on *WCW Nitro*, setting the tone for the "anything goes" ratings battle.

When Luger ditched his ego for old glory, he switched to star spangled trunks.

HEIGHT: 6 feet, 6 inches (198 cm)
WEIGHT: 275 pounds (125 kg)
HOMETOWN: Chicago, IL
SIGNATURE MOVE: Torture Rack

PHOTO FINISH

Lex Luger went the distance at the 1994 *Royal Rumble*, only he was not alone. Replay showed that Bret "Hit Man" Hart's feet hit the floor at the exact same time as his. With both Superstars pleading their case for a historic victory, the outcome was ruled a draw, setting up a controversial road to

LILIAN GARCIA

Lilian has honed her powerful singing voice since age five.

The most important tool of her trade, Lilian has a smile on her face whenever the mic is in her hand.

If Lilian Garcia is announcing your name, you know you have made it to the big time. Lilian's angelic vocal cords have accompanied WWE Superstars to the ring for well over a decade. She has welcomed the WWE Universe to the arena, explained match stipulations, and introduced the new title holder more times than she can remember. Her most cherished memories, though, are of belting out the Star-Spangled Banner to a rousing applause. She delivered a moving performance on *SmackDown* mere days after the tragedy of September 11th. Her emotional rendition of the anthem helped WWE to rally a grieving nation. Lilian always pours her heart into her singing, but there was something extra in her voice that night. Years later, Lilian took her musical chops outside WWE to record her own album. She didn't stay away long, however, and quickly returned. Her microphone was right where she left it.

POSITIONS HELD:
Raw Ring Announcer,
SmackDown Ring Announcer

U-S-A! U-S-A!
Lilian was twice given the honor of singing America the Beautiful to open *WrestleMania*. This puts her in some legendary company. Stars such as Aretha Franklin, Ray Charles, Willie Nelson, and others have sung this patriotic tune at the Showcase of the Immortals.

LUKE HARPER

Harper's bushy, thick beard is as black as his thoughts.

Luke Harper is one of the top three reasons to avoid the deep, dark wilderness. The other two, Erick Rowan and their terrifying patriarch, Bray Wyatt, lurk in the shadows beside him. This sadistic "family" has arrived, and no one in WWE should feel safe. Luke Harper does not say much. He leaves the sermonizing to his sinister leader and lets his savagery in the ring speak for itself. He and fellow follower Rowan carry out the family's disturbing vision of a future wrought with destruction. Wyatt's cryptic words are his bidding. He channels his imposing size and surprising agility on all naysayers to the cause. Little is known about where Harper first set himself on the path of the buzzards. One fact about this bizarre Superstar is crystal clear. Beneath those haunting eyes lie bad intentions. Those foolhardy enough to stare in the face of danger will suffer some callous consequences.

Harper delivers a backwoods beating in a plain white shirt, often with sleeveless flannel over the top.

The ring and the desolate woodlands are the same to Harper. He competes in the same jeans he wears at the family hideout.

HEIGHT: 6 feet, 5 inches (196 cm)

WEIGHT: 275 pounds (125 kg)

SCOUTING NEW MEMBERS

Luke Harper assisted Bray Wyatt in convincing Daniel Bryan to follow the buzzards in early 2014. After some forceful recruiting tactics, the Yes! Man enlisted. Though it turned out to be a façade by Bryan, Harper and company still gave the WWE Universe a glimpse of a fallen hero.

MANKIND

With his creepy mask, Mankind looks fit for the local nuthouse, but he has a heart of gold.

Mankind ascended from the boiler room during WWE's Attitude Era. On the surface this brooding outcast seemed destined for the mental ward. His raving lunacy and penchant for shoving his hands in opponents' mouths was off-putting at first. However, the future best-selling author showed why you never judge a book by its cover. He channeled the several personalities lurking behind his leather mask into one Hall of Famer. Years after witnessing Jimmy Snuka's leap off a Steel Cage, Mankind created his own infamous moment with an even higher cage. Not only did he survive a gruesome fall from atop the steel structure, he was standing and smiling through his shattered teeth moments later! The WWE Universe applauded his resiliency. Soon, the deranged madman became a lovable underdog with a gym sock for a companion. He went on to win the WWE Championship three times, reminding us all to "Have a nice day!"

HEIGHT: 6 feet, 2 inches (188 cm)

WEIGHT: 287 pounds (130 kg)

HOMETOWN: Long Island, NY

SIGNATURE MOVE:
Mandible Claw, Double Arm DDT

POSITIONS HELD:
WWE Commissioner, *Raw* Co-General Manager

Mankind ironically wore a tie with his tattered ensemble.

ROCK & SOCK

Years before Team Hell No, Mankind and The Rock formed an unlikely alliance. Despite a hellacious rivalry, the pugnacious People's Champ found a soft spot for his quirky counterpart. The polar opposites combined their strength to win multiple Tag Team Titles. Mankind even produced a tribute to The Rock called "This is Your Life." It was the highest rated segment in *Raw* history.

MARCUS LOUIS

Marcus Louis is a proud Frenchman who is ready to show the entire WWE Universe what his European homeland is all about. WWE fans have been no strangers to French Superstars throughout history, oftentimes having trouble getting on the same page as the foreign competitors. Whatever America's perception is, Louis is a legitimate tough guy. He played rugby as a young man and later joined the military, becoming a decorated riot police officer. Perhaps needing an even more dangerous job, he went on to work security in a psychiatric prison. Now, he and his partner Sylvester Lefort compete in NXT as The Legionnaires. Competing against other tough tag teams all fighting for a chance to reach the big time, the Legionnaires hold one French stereotype—arrogance. They believe they are superior to their American counterparts and plan to prove it.

> Marcus Louis waves a red, white, and blue flag in the ring—just not the one that NXT fans are typically apt to cheer.

HEIGHT: 6 feet, 2 inches (188 cm)

WEIGHT: 245 pounds (111 kg)

HOMETOWN: Bordeaux, France

COLD STREAK

Since defeating Jason Jordan and Mason Ryan to start their tag team run, The Legionnaires have not had the best of luck with The Ascension, El Local & Kalisto, and other teams. Louis has, however, defeated both Colin Cassady and Enzo Amore in singles action.

MARK HENRY

Mark Henry pulled off the impossible in 2013. He made himself look even more imposing by shaving his head bald.

Mark Henry's strength seems to grow with each passing year, a terrifying thought considering he has been the World's Strongest Man since most WWE Superstars were still in high school. First catching WWE's eye for his mammoth weightlifting prowess in international competitions, Henry has showcased his herculean power for over 15 years. Whether pulling two massive tractor trailers, bending a frying pan, or inducting another unfortunate Superstar into the Hall of Pain, Mark Henry does everything with swift brutality. Over the years, he has showcased several sides of his personality. He has also formed and broken several alliances along the way. This mountain of intimidation is best as his own man with his own pent up fury to guide his actions. When he fully unleashed his vicious nature in 2011, it led to the crowning achievement of his lengthy career. Henry won a long-overdue World Heavyweight Championship at Night of Champions.

Mark Henry's inescapable grasp can squeeze the air out of his adversaries like a boa constrictor.

HEIGHT: 6 feet, 4 inches (193 cm)

WEIGHT: 412 pounds (187 kg)

HOMETOWN: Silsbee, TX

SIGNATURE MOVES:
World's Strongest Slam

Emblems on Mark Henry's ring gear give a nod to his past as a champion power lifter.

WORLD'S STRONGEST SWERVE

In 2013, Mark Henry's tearful retirement speech led everyone, including John Cena, to believe he was calling it a career. It was all a ruse, however. The cunning colossus caught Cena with his guard down and flattened him with a World's

"MEAN" GENE OKERLUND

Mean Gene has perhaps the most illustrious mustache in WWE history.

Gene Okerlund always looked classy in his formal jacket and bowtie.

Gene Okerlund is one of the most enduring personalities in sports-entertainment history. In a career that spanned over thirty years, Okerlund delivered the scoop from behind the curtain, getting to the bottom of a story like no other. Affectionately nicknamed "Mean Gene" (or "Gene Mean" if you talk to Iron Sheik), his pointed questions and journalistic integrity earned him the respect of fans and Superstars alike. Mean Gene is forever linked to the Immortal Hulk Hogan. His unmistakable voice set up The Hulkster's most legendary pre-match pep talks. Gene has even joined Hogan for an amusing rendition of Hogan's signature pose down. Beyond rubbing elbows with icons, Mean Gene entertained as the host of *Tuesday Night Titans* and other talk shows. His incomparable blend of humor and intelligence kept the audience riveted to their sets. This Hall of Fame visionary makes the occasional return to WWE. His analysis is still as sharp as ever.

HOME: Minnesota

POSITIONS HELD: Locker room correspondent, Host of *All-American Wrestling, Tuesday Night Titans, Wrestling Challenge,* and *Prime Time Wrestling.*

BLAST FROM THE PAST

After eight years away from WWE, Gene Okerlund made his return at *WrestleMania X-Seven*. The 30-Man Gimmick Battle Royal featured several legendary Superstars, but the highlight of the match might have been two non-competitors. Mean Gene and Bobby Heenan formed the ultimate comedic combo, calling the action from ringside.

MICHAEL COLE

Michael Cole loves touting his multiple Slammy Awards, even the one he earned by losing his lunch in the middle of a broadcast.

Michael Cole has been calling the action in WWE for over a decade. Starting as a roving interviewer during the Attitude Era, the wars and elections he covered as a journalist more than prepared him for some sophomoric razzing from DX. Cole's hard-hitting questions landed him in the commentator's chair, where he now sits for every *Raw*, *SmackDown*, and pay-per-view. Perhaps from years of Superstars' verbal jabs or his own inflated ego, Cole can be insufferable at times. Claiming to have a massive fan base of "Cole-miners," he has fed this delusion by proclaiming himself the "Voice of WWE." He has also lashed out with venomous bias on occasion. His broadcast partner, Jerry "The King" Lawler, whipped him from pillar to post at *WrestleMania XXVII*. However, a controversial decision by the Anonymous *Raw* General Manager awarded Cole the victory. He can now boast a 1-0 record at *WrestleMania* … only 20 more wins to catch Undertaker!

Michael Cole always looks sharp, save for the absurd orange getup he wears when attempting to compete.

HOMETOWN:
Amenia, NY

POSITIONS HELD:
Raw commentator,
SmackDown commentator

EXCLUSIVE
Despite his transgressions, Cole is respected as a journalist. In recent years he has delivered revealing, riveting interviews with WWE COO Triple H. The WWE Universe has Cole to thank for this eye-opening look inside WWE. He has also entertained as co-host of the *JBL & Cole* Show on wwe.com.

"MILLION DOLLAR MAN" TED DIBIASE

DiBiase wore Custom made jackets from the finest tailors that money can buy.

The Million Dollar Man epitomized greed long before JBL or Alberto Del Rio bought their first limousine. DiBiase flaunted his lavish possessions and used his overflowing wallet to prove that "everybody has a price." He coerced fans to perform demeaning tasks for large sums of cash, from kissing his feet to barking like a dog. DiBiase's end game, however, was the WWE Championship. With the gargantuan Andre the Giant and a rogue referee on his payroll, he nearly pulled it off. Andre delivered the title as planned, but WWE brass refused the title change. Not to be outdone, DiBiase responded in true aristocratic fashion. He used his vast fortune to create his own diamond studded prize called the Million Dollar Championship. Satisfied at getting his way once again, he cackled his obnoxious, bellowing laughter all the way to the bank.

The gilded Million Dollar Championship, encrusted with real diamonds. Its legacy continued years later when DiBiase's son brought it back to WWE.

HEIGHT: 6 feet, 1 inch (185 cm)

WEIGHT: 260 pounds (118 kg)

HOMETOWN: Palm Beach, FL

SIGNATURE MOVE:
Million Dollar Dream

BANK ACCOUNT:
Infinite

SOLID INVESTMENTS

DiBiase's impact extends beyond his legendary persona and ring prowess. He unveiled Undertaker as part of his Million Dollar Team at *Survivor Series* 1990. Years later, he ushered Stone Cold Steve Austin into WWE—two rather impressive notches in his blinged out title belt.

MOJO RAWLEY

Mojo Rawley does not get hyped, he stays hyped. With this guiding principle, it will not be long before he is keeping his mojo up on the big stage in WWE. Now competing in NXT, Mojo brings an incredible amount of heart and desire to the ring. It is tough to wipe the smile off his face even when brawling with the toughest competition NXT has to offer. Mojo Rawley believes in passion, perseverance, and pride. These three P's served him well in his athletic career. Mojo was a dominant defensive tackle for the Maryland Terrapins and later patrolled the same position for the Green Bay Packers and Arizona Cardinals. His speed and strength overwhelmed opponents on the gridiron. Now a promising sports-entertainer, he is blasting ahead full speed looking to prove that he is the real deal. At *NXT ArRIVAL*, his explosive style was too much for CJ Parker.

Mojo Rawley's bright ring trunks display his mantra, "Stay Hyped" on the back.

Rawley takes his mojo to the ring, literally, with "MO" on one knee and "JO" on the other.

HEIGHT: 6 feet, 4 inches (193 cm)
WEIGHT: 290 pounds (132 kg)
HOMETOWN: Alexandra, VA
SIGNATURE MOVE: Hyperdrive

AN UNWELCOME ACCOLADE

Mojo Rawley made a valiant attempt to silence Rusev's anti-American diatribe at the first *NXT Takeover*. The Bulgarian Brute was ready for him and brutalized him with an Accolade submission hold. Though unsuccessful, Mojo earned respect for sticking up for America.

MR. MCMAHON

Donald Trump once shaved Mr. McMahon's famous hairdo after defeating him in a Battle of the Billionaires.

WWE is Mr. McMahon's world. Everyone else is just living in it. As Chairman and CEO, he is the supreme head honcho, ruthlessly guiding the course of his entertainment empire. He is brazen, calculating, and anything but modest. Who can blame him? For over 30 years he has transformed WWE into a global entertainment juggernaut, stomping out every threat to his mantle along the way. He has been humiliated by D-Generation X, blown up in his limousine, and challenged by deep-pocketed media mogul Ted Turner. Still, Mr. McMahon has emerged unscathed and spoiling for a fight. Some call him an evil genius. Others call him a business icon, but Mr. McMahon has no time for labels. He spends every waking moment plotting and planning new and innovative ways to entertain the WWE Universe, and fans respect him for it.

Mr. McMahon owns enough suits and ties to open his own Men's Warehouse franchise.

The boss means business with his patented power walk.

HOMETOWN: Greenwich, CT

POSITION: Chairman and CEO of WWE

CATCH PHRASE: YOU'RE FIRED!!

CAREER HIGHLIGHTS:
Chief innovator in sports-entertainment history, the creation of *WrestleMania*, epic rivalry with Stone Cold Steve Austin, squashing WCW in the Monday Night War, taking WWE public, and most recently, the groundbreaking WWE Network.

AFRAID? ... NO CHANCE IN HELL

Mr. McMahon is no ordinary business suit. He has the guts to step in the ring with some of the toughest Superstars in WWE history. The Chairman has been in brutal matches with Hulk Hogan, Undertaker, John Cena, Ric Flair, Bret Hart, Shawn Michaels, and many more.

MR. PERFECT

Mr. Perfect's golden locks were the reflection of perfection.

Mr. Perfect kept a wide spectrum of fluorescent singlets.

Whoever said "nobody's perfect" never met Curt Hennig. Most people dream of bowling the perfect game, blasting a towering home run, or sinking the impossible shot. Hennig could do all of this before breakfast just to remind us that he was what he claimed to be—absolutely perfect. A second-generation Superstar, Hennig crafted his flawless execution in his home state of Minnesota before adopting the "Perfect" moniker in WWE. Mr. Perfect raised the bar for technical wrestling even among the world's most elite. His tactical wizardry between the ropes earned him the Intercontinental Championship and made for some awe-inspiring battles with The Excellence of Execution, Bret Hart. Mr. Perfect did it all in WWE. From competing in the ring, to managing, to even describing the action as a commentator, Hennig did everything, you guessed it ...perfectly. He could have earned enshrinement in any Hall of Fame. Lucky for us, Curt Hennig chose WWE.

HEIGHT: 6 feet, 3 inches (191 cm)
WEIGHT: 257 pounds (117 kg)
HOMETOWN: Robbinsdale, MN
SIGNATURE MOVE: Perfectplex

Though white boots were his signature, Mr. Perfect could have made any color look impeccable.

LOSER LEAVES TOWN
Mr. Perfect served as the "Executive Consultant" to Ric Flair during Flair's two WWE Championship reigns, but tensions boiled over between Hennig and the Nature Boy. Flair may have boasted more hardware, but it was Perfect who got the last laugh. He bested Flair in a Loser Leaves Town Match in 1993, punching his former associate's ticket out of WWE.

NAOMI

Naomi is one of the fastest rising fireplugs in WWE. First shaking it for the WWE Universe as part of Brodus Clay's boogying entourage from Planet Funk, the curvaceous beauty has since stepped up her game in the Divas division. Whether on her own or with her former partner in funk, Cameron, Naomi has shown she is ready for the dance in more ways than one. Her in-ring agility and mettle have impressed her onlookers. At this rate, Naomi has potential to fill her WWE treasure chest with an incredible booty. With Tons of Funk firmly in her rear view, this shooting star continues to boost her profile across all sorts of platforms. She is part of the original cast of *Total Divas*, giving her fans an extra chance every week to get a glimpse of her fascinating world. As long as Naomi is here, the former Funkadactyls will never be far from the Divas Championship.

Naomi gets the max out of her gluteus maximus, using her famous feature to lay out her opponents in the ring with her signature move, the Rear View.

HEIGHT: 5 feet, 5 inches (165 cm)

HOMETOWN: Orlando, FL

SIGNATURE MOVES: Rear View

Naomi is extremely photogenic in her ring outfits, fashioned with glitter, tassels and other dazzling accessories.

CHANGING THEIR TUNE

Naomi and Cameron were not thrilled when Brodus Clay began to display a villainous streak on *Raw*. It spelled the end for Tons of Funk. The two Funkadactyls jumped ship to support the flashy duo of R-Truth and Xavier Woods before pursuing their own interests.

NATALYA

From dungeon to Diva, Natalya carries on the illustrious Hart family legacy in WWE. A feisty competitor, the daughter of Jim "The Anvil" Neidhart and niece of Bret "Hit Man" Hart combines the exalted qualities of her Hart Foundation forefathers. She competes with the same rough-and-tumble demeanor as her father, but can still execute her uncle's famed Sharpshooter with pink and black perfection. Aside from keeping family tradition alive, Natalya is resolute in her quest to leave her own stamp in WWE lore. Her never-ending goal is the Divas Championship. Since she first held the title in 2011, the butterfly has never been far from her grasp. Natalya is also an outspoken leader in the Divas' locker room, quick to lay a harsh reality check on any newbie who thinks Diva life is a cakewalk. Natalya is beautiful, tough, and determined—the embodiment of what it means to be a WWE Diva.

The Hart family is synonymous with Canada, as displayed by Natalya's pink heart set inside a Canadian maple leaf.

HEIGHT:
5 feet, 5 inches (165 cm)

HOMETOWN:
Calgary, Alberta

SIGNATURE MOVES:
Sharpshooter

A FAMILY THAT FIGHTS TOGETHER

Natalya aligned with her cousin David Hart Smith and future husband Tyson Kidd to form the Hart Dynasty. The last generation of dungeon grads displayed their Calgary-born chemistry in the ring. They also came to the aid of Bret Hart in his grudge match against Mr. McMahon at *WrestleMania XXVI*. Natalya even unleashed a slap on the embattled Chairman's fa   went he   ated!

NIKKI BELLA

Nikki and Brie Bella are of Italian and Mexican descent.

Nikki was always into athletics. She excelled at soccer before turning her attention to entertainment.

If traffic has come to a screeching halt, it might be The Bellas walking down the street. This double dose of Diva is not a hallucination. It's Nikki Bella and her twin sister, Brie. For years, these beautiful bombshells have turned heads and broken hearts in WWE, but do not dismiss them as eye candy. Whether tangling with other top Divas on their own or unleashing a little "Twin Magic," these spicy sisters spell double trouble for all their rivals. Nikki provided the assist when Brie Bella scored the first Divas Championship for the twin tandem. A year later, however, Nikki was able to strap the coveted title around her own waist after toppling the powerful Beth Phoenix. The hit show *Total Divas* provides a lens into Nikki's private life. This added attention has stirred jealousy among rival Divas, but Nikki and the rest of the cast have the skills to prove that they are not just pretty faces.

HEIGHT:
5 feet, 6 inches (168 cm)

HOMETOWN: Scottsdale, AZ

TANGLING TWINS

Nikki Bella and her sister, Brie, have each other's backs, but their sibling rivalry is always bound to surface. They once found themselves at odds over Daniel Bryan (ironically, Brie would say "I do" to The Beard years later). They also supported opposite teams in the battle of General Managers at *WrestleMania XXVIII*.

NIKOLAI VOLKOFF

A Soviet hammer and sickle was often emblazed on Volkoff's shirts.

Volkoff wore his signature furry head gear in support of the red army.

"Nikolai Volkoff would like us all to please rise and respect his singing of the Soviet National Anthem." That was the announcement that enraged crowds during this burly Russian's most memorable run in WWE. Volkoff teamed with another anti-American menace, Iron Sheik, to form a 1980's axis of evil in WWE. The foreign allies captured the Tag Team Titles and terrorized the popular US Express. Volkoff's body of work in WWE encompassed nearly four decades. Aside from his time with Iron Sheik, he enjoyed success as part of The Mongols, The Bolsheviks, and as a singles star. He even gave the incomparable Bruno Sammartino a tough test early in his career. But Volkoff will always be best remembered for his guttural rendition of the signature Soviet song and for showing the west just how evil his side of the Iron Curtain could be. For this, we stand and salute.

HEIGHT: 6 feet, 4 inches (193 cm)

WEIGHT: 313 pounds (142 kg)

HOMETOWN: The Soviet Union

SIGNATURE MOVE:
The Russian Backbreaker

CHANGE OF ALLIANCE

When the nation of Iraq emerged as America's enemy in the '90s, Volkoff underwent a surprising change of heart. He aligned with the patriotic "Hacksaw" Jim Duggan against Sgt. Slaughter, who had become an Iraqi sympathizer.

ONE MAN GANG

Skulls on One Man Gang's sleeves and the side of his head let everyone know he was dangerous.

One Man Gang wore a Mohawk similar to two other brawlers from Chicago, the Road Warriors.

Before unearthing his inner African soul, One Man Gang dressed as if he just stepped off a Harley.

One man, two distinct personas, and countless flattened opponents staring at the ceiling—that was the career of One Man Gang. A grizzly street thug always looking for a knockdown, drag out brawl, One Man Gang served the crooked agenda of his oily manager, Slick. As mean as they come, One Man Gang couldn't care less if you were a Superstar, referee, or anyone else. If you had a heartbeat, you were a target for a pounding by the big man. The chaos continued through one of the most memorable transformations in WWE history. Under Slick's tutelage, One Man Gang was reborn as Akeem "The African Dream." Clad in blue and yellow with distinct African patterns, the rechristened brawler unleashed his inner soul, adding a little boogie to his beat downs. Akeem danced his way out of WWE in the '90s, but not before contributing to the Megapowers' break up.

HEIGHT: 6 feet, 9 inches (206 cm)
WEIGHT: 450 pounds (204 kg)
HOMETOWN: Chicago, IL
SIGNATURE MOVE: 747 Splash

TWIN TOWERS
Akeem and Big Boss Man matched their incredible mass to form the Twin Towers. With the former prison guard by his side, Akeem enjoyed knocking around the best tag teams in WWE until a beef caused the two friends to collide at *WrestleMania VI*.

PAIGE

> Don't let her enchanting beauty fool you.
> Paige can kick your head in.

Paige holds the accolade of being the youngest woman to ever hold the Divas Championship, but if you think she took a shortcut to the big stage, you are sorely mistaken. The British competitor has prepared her entire life for this chance, first lacing up at the tender age of thirteen. Competing in NXT, the determined newcomer showcased a ring savvy beyond her years and a mean streak that garnered high praise from fellow Brit, William Regal. Her impressive showing earned her the chance to prove herself on a higher level. No one could have expected the shocker that unfolded on her arrival. Goaded into a championship match by AJ Lee, the feisty new Diva pulled off what no Diva could do for 295 days, pinning the boastful champion. Refusing to rest on her laurels, Paige continues to polish her skills and is primed to be the "Diva of Tomorrow."

HEIGHT: 5 feet, 8 inches (173 cm)

HOMETOWN: Norwich, England

SIGNATURE MOVE:
Paige-Turner, Ram-Paige,
PTO (Paige Tap Out)

EXTREME TEST

Defending the Diva's Championship for the first time against Tamina, many expected Paige's unlikely reign to be cut short. At Extreme Rules, she stepped up and forced the dangerous Diva to submit to the Scorpion Crosslock. Though AJ would eventually end her first title reign, Paige proved that she is here to stay.

PAPA SHANGO

Papa Shango's face looked like the visage of death, one of the most horrifying images in WWE history.

Papa Shango's bone necklace and skull, which billowed an eerie cloud of smoke, were a necessity in casting evil spells over WWE.

Papa Shango was a master of black magic who haunted all WWE's top Superstars during his brief but memorable reign of terror in 1992. The mystical voodoo priest's most infamous moment came at the expense of the Ultimate Warrior. During a bizarre interview, an apparent spell cast by Shango caused a strange black liquid to ooze from Warrior's head. The incident served as the exclamation point to his supernatural stint in WWE. The magic man with the unnerving skeletal face paint also caused a disruption during the main event of *WrestleMania VIII* that lead to Sid Justice being disqualified. Beyond the magic, Papa Shango was a physical competitor capable of putting down the spell book and using his muscular frame to leave opponents lying in defeat. Though he vanished seemingly into thin air, Papa Shango is still a shining example that anything is possible in WWE.

HEIGHT: 6 feet, 6 inches (198 cm)

WEIGHT: 330 pounds (150 kg)

HOMETOWN: Parts Unknown

SIGNATURE MOVE: Shoulder Breaker

SPELL REVERSED

By the time Papa Shango made his first *Royal Rumble* appearance, it appeared the magic had run out. Shango was tossed from the ring in less than thirty seconds and was out of WWE shortly afterward.

PAUL BEARER

Paul Bearer's golden urn possessed cosmic power, and also came in han as a foreign object.

Paul Bearer's pallid complexion is the mark of a lifetime spent in darkness.

Paul Bearer managed the most illustrious client in the history of managers, Undertaker. Bearer supplanted Brother Love when The Deadman needed a more ghoulish guide to set him on his path of destruction. With the power of his mystical urn, Bearer channeled Undertaker's phenomenal abilities in the ring. Before you can say "Rest in Peace," WWE's top Superstars were sleeping with one eye open, frightful of this terrifying tandem. Paul Bearer dwelled in an eerie Funeral Parlor that housed the final resting place for his client's victims. Here, he contemplated matters of the morbid and spoke to the WWE Universe in haunting, high-pitched tones. His unnerving delivery could make a Dr. Seuss book sound like a campfire story from hell. This unique way of striking the senses added to Undertaker's legendary mystique. Now, legend has it that on stormy nights, the shrill sound of "Oh yeeess" can be heard through the dimly lit walls of the WWE Hall of Fame.

HEIGHT: 5 feet, 10 inches (178 cm)

SUPERSTARS MANAGED:
Undertaker, Kane, Mankind

ALL IN THE FAMILY

Paul Bearer and Undertaker were not always on the same side of the graveyard fence. Bearer literally unleashed hell on The Deadman when he brought his half-brother Kane into WWE. For years, Bearer was the evil puppet master in this sordid sibling rivalry.

PAUL HEYMAN

Whether singing his client's praises or inciting the crowd, Heyman's words always get under the skin.

This evil genius is always one step ahead, and only he knows his true motives.

Paul Heyman may not be big, strong, or the slightest bit athletic, but he is still one highly dangerous man. A product of the Big Apple with the attitude to show for it, Heyman possesses the two most lethal weapons in sports-entertainment: a razor sharp tongue and a scheming mind. Heyman's next move is anybody's guess. He concocts each devious plot with the delightful wickedness of a mad scientist. Despite this notorious reputation, his services are always in high demand. Nobody advocates for his clients with more tenacity than Heyman. Since CM Punk proudly injected the term "Paul Heyman Guy" into WWE lingo, a convoy of Superstars has made this deal with the devil to bolster their careers. The Second City Saint himself enjoyed most of his 434 day title reign under Heyman's watchful eye. Of course, Heyman's most infamous success story is Brock Lesnar, the Beast who broke Undertaker's iconic winning streak at *WrestleMania*.

HOMETOWN: Scarsdale, NY

POSITIONS HELD:
SmackDown General Manager

SUPERSTARS MANAGED:
Brock Lesnar, Cesaro, CM Punk, Curtis Axel, Big Show, Kurt Angle

EXTREME REVOLUTION

Aside from his exploits as a duplicitous Superstar advocate, many fans respect Paul Heyman as the brains behind Extreme Championship Wrestling. Heyman's innovative thinking catapulted the smalltime promotion to a national stage. ECW's edgy, hardcore style helped influence WWE's lauded Attitude Era.

PAUL ORNDORFF

Even when concealed behind one of his flowing robes, Orndorff's physique looked like a mountain of rock solid muscle.

Not much can be said about Paul Orndorff that he has not already said about himself. A Superstar ahead of his time, Orndorff was the personification of arrogance and excellence. He called himself "Mr. Wonderful," and with his physique and raw skill, who can argue? It came as no surprise that Roddy Piper saw Orndorff as the perfect partner to bring to battle against Hulk Hogan and Mr. T in the main event of the first *WrestleMania*. This was not the last time Orndorff butted heads with the Hulkster. The two tanned, chiseled warriors met on *Saturday Night's Main Event* inside the blocky, blue confines of WWE's classic Steel Cage. The match was hard-hitting and memorable, just like Orndorff himself. "Mr Wonderful" laid the groundwork for several generations to follow and dedicated his life after WWE to molding future stars, leading to a deserved Hall of Fame induction in 2005.

At the conclusion of Orndorff's famous Cage Match with Hulk Hogan, controversy broke out when it appeared both Superstars' feet touched the floor at the same time.

HEIGHT: 6 feet (183 cm)

WEIGHT: 252 pounds (114 kg)

HOMETOWN: Brandon, FL

SIGNATURE MOVE: Piledriver

FRACTURED FRIENDSHIP

Though "Cowboy" Bob Orton's miscue was the culprit in the team's *WrestleMania* loss, Roddy Piper blamed Orndorff. The Hot Rod's finger pointing ignited a bitter rivalry that caused Orndorff to join forces with Piper's nemesis, Hulk Hogan, for a brief time.

R-TRUTH

R-Truth grabs the microphone for ringside rhyming or just speaking the truth.

R-Truth has one burning question on his mind: "What's up?!" But one look into his maniacal eyes will tell you that a whole world of bizarre lunacy lurks at the end of the rabbit hole. The most troublesome fixture of his wild imagination is Little Jimmy, whose image Truth first projected on the faces of spectators. The wacky Superstar blamed the "Jimmys" for shortcomings in his career. Over time, this deranged paranoia wore off and Little Jimmy evolved into his invisible, pint sized pal at ringside. Whether rapping his energetic entrance theme on his own or with a make believe toddler in tow, R-Truth is sure to bring the entertainment to a blistering pace. He leaves nothing in the locker room, competing with the same zany enthusiasm that he uses on the microphone. The truth, as he says, has set him free. Now a veteran, this free-spirited Superstar is as unpredictable as ever.

R-Truth has his first initial inked on his chest.

Jeans decked in graffiti give R-Truth a gritty, street look.

HEIGHT: 6 feet, 2 inches (188 cm)

WEIGHT: 220 pounds (100 kg)

HOMETOWN: Charlotte, NC

SIGNATURE MOVES: Lie Detector

TAG TEAM TURMOIL

R-Truth and The Miz once took aim at perceived injustices in WWE. Dubbed The Awesome Truth, the two bitter Superstars made a formidable tandem until felled by The Rock and John Cena at *Survivor Series*. The following year, Truth found a kindred spirit in Kofi Kingston. This aerial alliance enjoyed a reign with the Tag Team Championships.

RANDY "MACHO MAN" SAVAGE

Savage only removed his wraparound sunglasses to compete in the ring.

The Macho Man's closet featured a never-ending spectrum of colors.

Randy Savage embodied the raging '80s in WWE. With his often-imitated cadence, flamboyant outfits, and over the top interviews, Macho Man's style was only outshined by his athleticism. His surprising hire of manager Miss Elizabeth shot his career to the stratosphere. Despite his boorish demeanor, Savage and Elizabeth became WWE's original power couple. Their crowning achievements came on WWE's grandest stage. At *WrestleMania III*, Macho Man made history in defeat when he and Ricky Steamboat delivered a jaw-dropping performance for the WWE Universe. A year later, he won an amazing four matches in one night to take home the gold in the historic WWE Championship Tournament. Macho Madness reigned supreme in WWE, and this uniquely charismatic and dynamic Superstar is still revered to this day.

HEIGHT:
6 feet, 2 inches (188 cm)

WEIGHT:
237 pounds (108 kg)

HOMETOWN:
Sarasota, FL

SIGNATURE MOVE:
Elbow Drop

CATCH PHRASE:
OH YEAH!!

THE MEGA POWERS
Randy Savage and Hulk Hogan formed an awesome combination known as The Mega Powers. Jealously eventually drove a wedge in this union, however. The duo officially "exploded" at *WrestleMania V*, with Savage losing the WWE Championship to Hogan.

RANDY ORTON

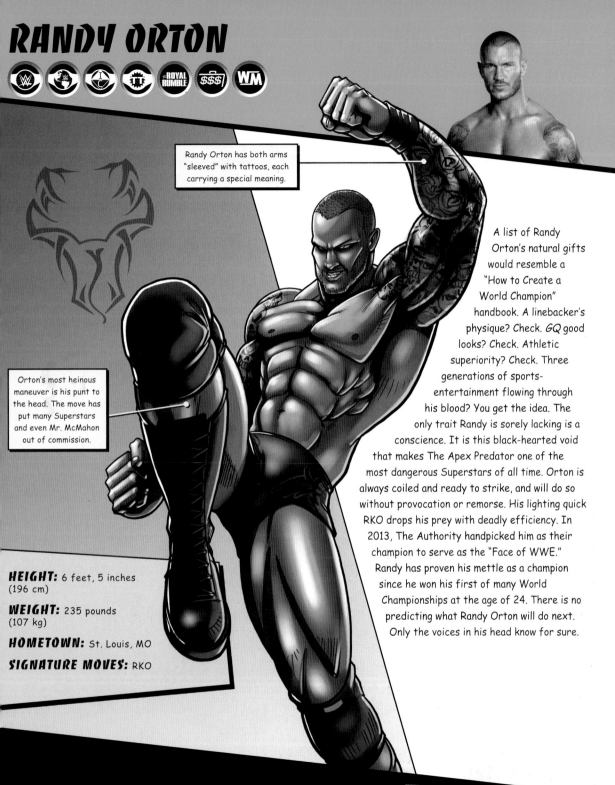

Randy Orton has both arms "sleeved" with tattoos, each carrying a special meaning.

Orton's most heinous maneuver is his punt to the head. The move has put many Superstars and even Mr. McMahon out of commission.

A list of Randy Orton's natural gifts would resemble a "How to Create a World Champion" handbook. A linebacker's physique? Check. *GQ* good looks? Check. Athletic superiority? Check. Three generations of sports-entertainment flowing through his blood? You get the idea. The only trait Randy is sorely lacking is a conscience. It is this black-hearted void that makes The Apex Predator one of the most dangerous Superstars of all time. Orton is always coiled and ready to strike, and will do so without provocation or remorse. His lighting quick RKO drops his prey with deadly efficiency. In 2013, The Authority handpicked him as their champion to serve as the "Face of WWE." Randy has proven his mettle as a champion since he won his first of many World Championships at the age of 24. There is no predicting what Randy Orton will do next. Only the voices in his head know for sure.

HEIGHT: 6 feet, 5 inches (196 cm)

WEIGHT: 235 pounds (107 kg)

HOMETOWN: St. Louis, MO

SIGNATURE MOVES: RKO

DUAL DESTINIES

Randy Orton and John Cena's deep-seated rivalry began over a decade ago. Their careers have shared eerie parallels, often reaching similar milestones at the same time. Of their many championship showdowns, none were as monumental as *TLC 2013*. In a grueling battle, Orton defeated Cena to become the inaugural WWE World Heavyweight Champion.

RAZOR RAMON

One curly strand of hair swayed between Razor's eyes, daring you to look at him cross-eyed.

Razor's loud vests were a signature of his bad boy style.

Razor's gold chains would weigh down an average sized man.

...Hey yo. Razor Ramon redefined "cool" in WWE. With thick gold chains dangling around his neck, oily black hair, and a toothpick dancing between his teeth, Razor oozed machismo from every pore in his body. He was ill-mannered, quick tempered, and boorish. In an age when people still gravitated toward straight laced, cartoonish do-gooders, he was "The Bad Guy." Razor's edgy persona challenged the status quo. The more he flicked his toothpick in people's faces, the more he became a guilty pleasure for fans who discovered their inner bad boy. It was fun to cheer for Razor, never more so than at *WrestleMania X* when he and Shawn Michaels created a masterpiece in a Ladder Match for the ages. Razor fully went rogue in 1996, bringing the New World Order to WCW. Now, he is no longer an Outsider to the WWE Hall of Fame. "The Bad Guy" received his overdue honor in 2014.

Images of actual razors were emblazoned on Ramon's knee pads.

HEIGHT: 6 feet, 7 inches (201 cm)

WEIGHT: 287 pounds (130 kg)

HOMETOWN: Miami, FL

SIGNATURE MOVE: Razor's Edge

YOU WANT A WAR?

Razor Ramon committed one of the most brazen moves in history. On an episode of *Monday Nitro*, Razor walked into the WCW ring like he owned the place. His ensuing speech stoked the fires in the Monday Night War. For the rest of his career, he and the n.W.o did "what they want, when they want."

RENEE YOUNG

Renee Young brings a rare mix of beauty and brains to WWE's on-air broadcasting team.

Renee Young is used to interviewing Superstars and Divas after a victory, but after breaking ground as a female commentator on *WWE Superstars*, it was Renee's turn to tout her accomplishment. She expressed excitement over the opportunity to call the action she grew up watching.

Renee Young is a bright, energetic broadcaster who comes to WWE from Toronto, Canada, a city rich in sports-entertainment history. Having honed her journalistic skills in the local Canadian sports scene, Renee's vibrant personality has brought a breath of fresh air to WWE's backstage interviews. Renee is a go-getter, not shy about seeking out the exclusive story from WWE's most intimidating stars. She blends the enthusiasm of a lifelong WWE Universe member with the buttoned up demeanor of a seasoned pro. With broadcasting chops beyond her years, is Renee destined to be the first female color commentator on *Raw* or *SmackDown*? Fans who watch *NXT* might think so. The Canadian beauty has taken a seat at the NXT announcers' table to call the matches of WWE's future stars. Get used to this driven young maven of the mic. She has the potential to become a fixture on WWE airwaves.

HEIGHT: 5 feet, 5 inches (165 cm)
HOMETOWN: Toronto, Ontario

INTERNET SENSATION

In addition to her many responsibilities on *Raw, SmackDown,* and *NXT,* Renee Young is a featured correspondent on the popular JBL & Cole web show.

Rey conceals his face, following sacred lucha libre tradition. He owns several hundred masks in a never-ending variety of colors.

Whoever decided that size matters failed to tell Rey Mysterio. WWE's masked avenger from the 619 has been making jaws drop for two decades in sports-entertainment. What Rey lacks in height, he makes up tenfold in guts, guile, and athleticism. Staring up at his opponents, the Ultimate Underdog defies odds and gravity. His innovative aerial assaults level the playing field against WWE's massive Superstars. Few can keep up with his dizzying pace in the ring. Seeming to invent moves in mid-air, he baffles his rivals as he sets them up for his illustrious 619 finisher. Since taking flight at the age of fifteen in Mexico, he has kept spectators on the edge of their seats. Mysterio has overcome the cruel "tale of the tape" countless times. His dimensions may not measure up to the big boys, but his trophy case certainly does. In his lengthy career, he has claimed nearly every prize there is to win, earning his nickname "The Biggest Little Man."

Several tats represent all that is near and dear to Rey, from his two kids to his heritage, history, and faith.

HEIGHT: 5 feet, 6 inches (168 cm)

WEIGHT: 175 pounds (79 kg)

HOMETOWN:
San Diego, CA

SIGNATURE MOVE:
619, West Coast Pop

UNDERDOG CHAMPION

Rey's greatest run began at the 2006 *Royal Rumble*, where he survived over an hour of competition to advance to *WrestleMania*. At the Show of Shows, he shocked the world by winning the World Heavyweight Championship in a whirlwind Triple Threat Match. His victory became an inspiration for athletes of all sizes to dream big.

RIC FLAIR

Platinum blond hair is part of Flair's signature style.

The Nature Boy's majestic robes cost more than the average car.

"Nature Boy" Ric Flair is a limousine riding, jet flying legend of sports-entertainment. Animated and full of red-faced intensity, "Slick Ric" spent over three decades proving his eternal reminder that "To be the man, you gotta beat the man." With slicked blonde hair, sequined robes and an unmistakable strut, he projected grandeur with every step he took. Men wanted to be him. Women wanted to be next to him. In the ring, he famously boasts an astounding sixteen World Championships, all after breaking his back in a plane crash. Flair earned a reputation as "the dirtiest player in the game" with sneaky tactics that were both infuriating and endearing to the audience. Today, the WWE Universe trumpets his arrival with an appreciative "Woooooo!" whenever he styles and profiles for the masses.

HEIGHT:
6 feet, 1 inch (185 cm)

WEIGHT:
243 pounds (110 kg)

HOMETOWN: Charlotte, NC

SIGNATURE MOVE:
Figure-Four Leg Lock

CATCH PHRASE:
"Woooooo!"

IV
Ric Flair joined forces with Arn Anderson, Ole Anderson, and Tully Blanchard to form The Four Horsemen. The dominant stable set the benchmark for D-Generation X, The Shield, and countless others to follow.

RICK RUDE

Rick Rude often stole a kiss from a female audience member, giving her a taste of his caterpillar mustache.

When "Ravishing" Rick Rude removed his robe to show off his sculpted physique, he looked as if he were ripped from the cover of a tawdry romance novel. Rude's swiveling hips and rippling abs made the ladies weak in the knees, even if WWE's resident hunk was an insufferable boor. Rick Rude was so full of himself he demanded silence while he unclothed for the camera. He derided his spectators, referring to them as "sweat hogs" for not living up to his impossible standard of fitness. If Rick Rude hogged anything himself, it was attention. The flashing cameras blended with sounds of catcalls and boos fueled his success in the ring. Many of WWE's top contenders were in for a "Rude Awakening" once this brash Superstar got down to business. His calculated head games and stellar athleticism earned him the Intercontinental Title, giving the ladies one more thing on which to feast their eyes.

Rick Rude sometimes gained a psychological edge by airbrushing his foes' faces on his tights. One night, he crossed a line by displaying the image of Jake Robert's wife, infuriating "The Snake."

HEIGHT: 6 feet, 3 inches (191 cm)

WEIGHT: 252 pounds (114 kg)

HOMETOWN: Robbinsdale, MN

SIGNATURE MOVE:
Rude Awakening

INSURANCE POLICY
Later in his career, Rick Rude traded in his sparkling robes for a suit and a briefcase to serve as the "insurance policy" for the original D-Generation X

RICKY "THE DRAGON" STEAMBOAT

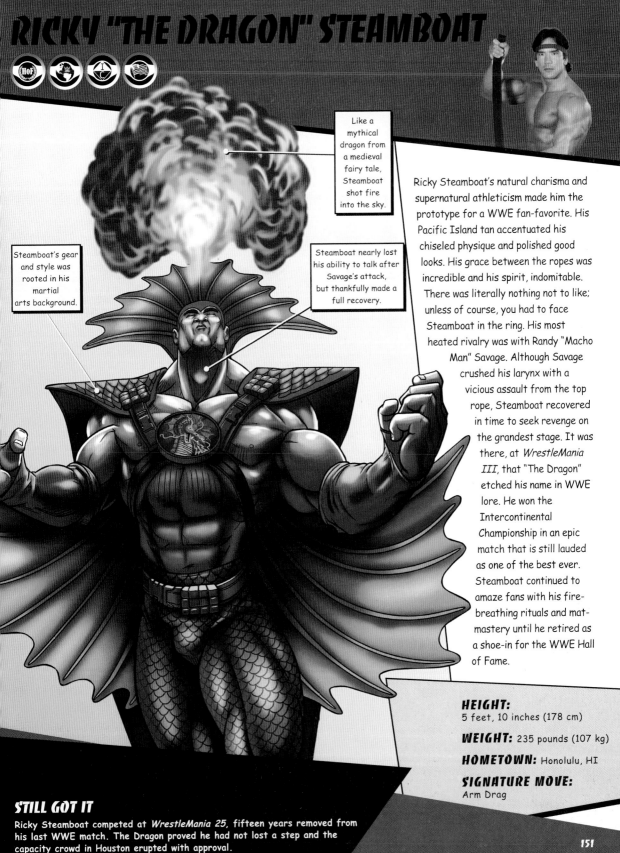

Like a mythical dragon from a medieval fairy tale, Steamboat shot fire into the sky.

Steamboat's gear and style was rooted in his martial arts background.

Steamboat nearly lost his ability to talk after Savage's attack, but thankfully made a full recovery.

Ricky Steamboat's natural charisma and supernatural athleticism made him the prototype for a WWE fan-favorite. His Pacific Island tan accentuated his chiseled physique and polished good looks. His grace between the ropes was incredible and his spirit, indomitable. There was literally nothing not to like; unless of course, you had to face Steamboat in the ring. His most heated rivalry was with Randy "Macho Man" Savage. Although Savage crushed his larynx with a vicious assault from the top rope, Steamboat recovered in time to seek revenge on the grandest stage. It was there, at *WrestleMania III*, that "The Dragon" etched his name in WWE lore. He won the Intercontinental Championship in an epic match that is still lauded as one of the best ever. Steamboat continued to amaze fans with his fire-breathing rituals and mat-mastery until he retired as a shoe-in for the WWE Hall of Fame.

HEIGHT:
5 feet, 10 inches (178 cm)

WEIGHT: 235 pounds (107 kg)

HOMETOWN: Honolulu, HI

SIGNATURE MOVE:
Arm Drag

STILL GOT IT

Ricky Steamboat competed at *WrestleMania 25*, fifteen years removed from his last WWE match. The Dragon proved he had not lost a step and the capacity crowd in Houston erupted with approval.

ROAD DOGG JESSE JAMES

"Oh you didn't know?" It's that D-O-Double G, the Road Dogg Jesse James. Road Dogg's motor mouth provided the soundtrack for D-Generation X during the Attitude Era. Brash and defiant, the Dogg lifted his leg on the rulebook. The more disobedient he became, the more WWE fans rallied behind him. His self-introductions alongside Billy Gunn became rock concerts. Capacity crowds barked along with him, echoing the arrival of the FIVE-TIME TAG TEAM CHAMPIONS OF THE WOOOOORLD, The NEW. AGE. OUTLAWS! Then the chaos began. The Outlaws' debauchery had no bounds. Just ask Cactus Jack and Chainsaw Charlie, who were tossed off the stage in a dumpster. Today, the scar Road Dogg left on the establishment still remains. If you think he is done, you better call somebody. Like a bad penny, the Outlaws returned to terrorize the Tag Team division in 2013, shocking the world by claiming a sixth Tag Team Title.

Road Dogg often competed in a loose-fitting, football style jersey.

Road Dogg has clipped his braids from the '90s but is still just as wild.

HEIGHT: 6 feet, 1 inch (185 cm)

WEIGHT: 241 pounds (109 kg)

HOMETOWN: Marietta, GA

SIGNATURE MOVE:
Shake, Rattle & Roll

HIS OWN DOGG

Road Dogg is best known for causing a ruckus with the Outlaws, but he was also an accomplished singles star. The lawless landscape of WWE's Hardcore Championship scene played right into his paws. He also enjoyed a reign with the prestigious Intercontinental Title.

ROAD WARRIOR ANIMAL

Skin on the bottom, one narrow strip on top. Animal's tough-guy appearance was not just a hairstyle. It was a lifestyle.

When Animal's face was painted, he was headed for battle. It was wise to get out of his way.

With signature spikes gleaming from atop their shoulder pads, The Road Warriors' presence spelled doom.

The Road Warriors pillaged and plundered everywhere they stopped in their two decade journey through sports-entertainment. WWE was no different. Animal is one half of this legendary team, the most decorated and dominant in the history of tag teams. Burly, ornery, and street tough, Animal brought a rough Chicago style to the ring. The spiked shoulder pads and intimidating war paint topped with a fierce Mohawk told opponents all they needed to know. When Animal and his partner Hawk stepped through the ropes, they were not there for a wrestling match; they were there for a brawl. Their Doomsday Device finishing move was devastating and earned them countless titles. Hawk's clothesline alone was vicious. With the target thrust six feet off the ground on Animal's mighty shoulders, there was no escape. Some of WWE's most fabled tag teams found this out the hard way.

HEIGHT: 6 feet, 2 inches (188 cm)

WEIGHT: 305 pounds (138 kg)

HOMETOWN: Chicago, IL

SIGNATURE MOVE: Doomsday Device

COMEBACK

Road Warrior Animal returned to WWE in 2005. After several years away, he had not lost a step. Though attempted partnerships did not recapture the magic he shared with Hawk, a new generation has introduced the Road Warrior brand of chaos. The future Hall of Famer even went solo for a brief stretch before hanging up his shoulder pads. Oh, what a rush!

Hawk shaved the top of his head. With Animal sporting a Mohawk, it looked as though the teammates could plug into each other.

Spiked shoulder pads helped make The Road Warriors the most recognizable and intimidating team in history.

Hawk used a variety of face paint patterns, each equally intimidating.

Oh, what a rush! Road Warrior Hawk's signature line said it all. The Road Warriors were an instant shot of adrenalin for all who witnessed their rampage through sports-entertainment. Hawk was battle tested on the mean streets of Chicago. Once he found a kindred spirit in Animal, this rough-and-tumble Superstar never looked back. He became one half of The Road Warriors, aka The Legion of Doom. Together, Hawk and Animal laid waste to anyone who stood in their path. They amassed a collection of gold worthy of Fort Knox, collecting Tag Team Titles in several different promotions. In WWE, they collided with legendary duos such as the Hart Foundation and the New Age Outlaws. Hawk's gruff way of speaking is often imitated, never duplicated. His gravelly interviews are as legendary as the mayhem that followed. With their combined power, The Road Warriors set the benchmark by which all tag teams are judged.

HEIGHT: 6 feet, 3 inches (191 cm)
WEIGHT: 270 pounds (122 kg)
HOMETOWN: Chicago, IL
SIGNATURE MOVE: Doomsday Device

CHICAGO STREET *FIGHT*

The Legion of Doom had the home field advantage at *WrestleMania 13*, and it showed. Despite being blasted by many foreign objects, Hawk and Animal prevailed over the Nation of Domination.

ROB VAN DAM

Rob Van Dam is truly "one of a kind." With martial arts, acrobatics, and death defying stunts working in Zen-like harmony, his matches are the ultimate thrill ride. While some say these tactics pose as much danger to himself as to his opponents, the results speak for themselves. Out of several Superstars to join WWE from the Land of Extreme, RVD is by far the most successful. He has spun, flipped, and leaped his way to an abundance of championships, all with the cool temperament of one who is just "chilling out." With over a decade of WWE experience, RVD comes and goes from the spotlight, picking his battles. When the time comes, you can be sure the WWE Universe will have their two thumbs cocked and ready for a chant of "Rob! Van! Dam!"

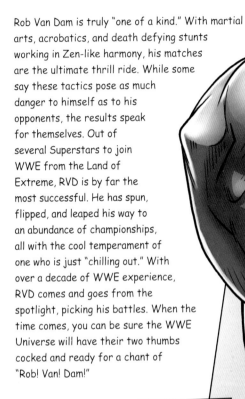

HEIGHT: 6 feet (183 cm)

WEIGHT: 235 pounds (107 kg)

HOMETOWN: Battle Creek, MI

NICKNAMES:
Mr. Monday Night, The Whole Dam Show

SIGNATURE MOVE:
Five Star Frog Splash, Van Terminator, Rolling Thunder

RVD has a limitless array of colorful singlets. Each harkens to his martial arts background.

RVD is extremely flexible, able to do a full sideways split while holding a dumbbell against his midsection. He calls this the Van Dam lift.

ECW

Rob Van Dam is a celebrated ECW original. The extreme promotion redefined sports-entertainment for its rabid followers in the 1990s. Years later, nothing delighted the hardcore faithful more than RVD's pinning of John Cena in front of a partisan New York City crowd.

ROCKY JOHNSON

Rocky Johnson was as charismatic as they come, rallying crowds with his good looks, athleticism, and personality. Sound familiar? It should. Years later, his son used these same traits to become The Most Electrifying Man in All of Entertainment. Lucky for The Rock, he had the advantage of learning from one of the best. The senior Rocky was a legend in his own right and a pioneer. He was as smooth as silk in the ring, with the most graceful and devastating Drop Kick ever seen. As a showman, Johnson was unequalled, flashing his fancy footwork as he battled for championship glory. Johnson altered history for the better when he and Tony Atlas became the first black men to capture the Tag Team Titles. This groundbreaking moment is still celebrated today. It is one of the many reasons why Johnson joined the WWE Hall of Fame, inducted by his son, in 2008.

Rocky Johnson knew what it took to build a rock solid physique. He did not take it easy on The Rock when training his son for the ring.

Johnson often had his initials "RJ" etched on his trunks.

HEIGHT: 6 feet, 2 inches (188 cm)
WEIGHT: 260 pounds (118 kg)
HOMETOWN: Toronto, Ontario
SIGNATURE MOVE: Drop Kick

GENERATIONS ALIGN

After The Rock pinned The Sultan in his *WrestleMania* debut, Iron Sheik and the rest of The Sultan's entourage attacked him. That was when the elder Johnson rushed to his son's aid to fend off the attackers. Rocky Johnson and son proved at *WrestleMania 13* that you do not cross one of WWE's most illustrious families.

"ROWDY" RODDY PIPER

"Just when you think you have all the answers, I change the questions!"

As WWE's original loud mouth, "Rowdy" Roddy Piper never had an opinion that he kept to himself. His revolutionary and controversial talk show, *Piper's Pit,* provided the platform for his outspoken venom. He berated his guests with verbal barbs... if they were lucky. The unlucky ones received a blindsided attack or, in Jimmy Snuka's case, a coconut-loaded haymaker to the skull. Notorious incidents such as this punctuated Piper's career. However, the Hot Rod's biggest impact in WWE came as the antithesis to Hulk Hogan and the "Rock n' Wrestling" movement. His conflict with the Hulkster, Mr. T, and others drew national attention. Piper headlined the first *WrestleMania* and though his team lost, his legacy remains as the scourge of the '80s in WWE.

Piper's ringed t-shirt with his HOT ROD! emblem is still popular with the WWE Universe.

Don't call it a skirt. It's a kilt, worn with pride like a true Scotsman.

HEIGHT: 6 feet, 2 inches (188 cm)

WEIGHT: 230 Lbs (104 kg)

HOMETOWN:
Glasgow, Scotland

SIGNATURE MOVE:
Sleeper Hold

A TASTE OF GOLD

After nearly a decade, Piper finally took home some WWE hardware when he usurped The Mountie for the Intercontinental Championship in 1992.

ROMAN REIGNS

Roman Reigns was first unleashed on WWE as the muscle-bound enforcer for The Shield. The Hounds of Justice inflicted a trail of wreckage across the landscape worthy of the n.W.o and the Fabulous Freebirds. Reigns served as the trio's tower of force, intimidating with his presence and strong enough to impose his will on any detractors to their cause. The Shield may have disbanded, but Reigns is just getting started. He has all the tools, even down to his genetic make-up, to be a serious World Championship juggernaut for years to come. He is built like his cousin, The Rock, with a mean streak akin to his Samaon ancestors. He competes with the same ferocity that made him a stand out college football player. The WWE Universe has taken notice. Since rebelling against The Authority, Reigns has exploded in popularity, his momentum gaining like a massive boulder rolling downhill towards an unfortunate target.

HEIGHT: 6 feet, 3 inches (191 cm)

WEIGHT: 265 pounds (120 kg)

HOMETOWN: Pensacola, FL

SIGNATURE MOVE: Spear, Superman Punch

Reigns still gives a nod to The Shield with his imposing black riot gear.

Roman Reigns launches himself in the air before connecting with his devastating Superman Punch.

RUMBLE RECORD

Roman Reigns showcased his dominance at the 2014 *Royal Rumble*. Though he did not win the 30-Man Battle Royal, he eliminated over one third of the participants. Reigns broke Kane's previous record, tossing twelve men over the top rope. This is not the worst thing Roman has done to Kane. He and The Shield made life miserable

RON SIMMONS

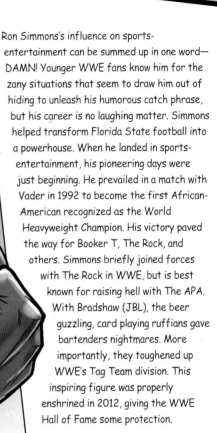

Ron Simmons was gifted with natural power and is revered as one of the toughest competitors of all time.

Ron Simmons's influence on sports-entertainment can be summed up in one word—DAMN! Younger WWE fans know him for the zany situations that seem to draw him out of hiding to unleash his humorous catch phrase, but his career is no laughing matter. Simmons helped transform Florida State football into a powerhouse. When he landed in sports-entertainment, his pioneering days were just beginning. He prevailed in a match with Vader in 1992 to become the first African-American recognized as the World Heavyweight Champion. His victory paved the way for Booker T, The Rock, and others. Simmons briefly joined forces with The Rock in WWE, but is best known for raising hell with The APA. With Bradshaw (JBL), the beer guzzling, card playing ruffians gave bartenders nightmares. More importantly, they toughened up WWE's Tag Team division. This inspiring figure was properly enshrined in 2012, giving the WWE Hall of Fame some protection.

HEIGHT: 6 feet, 2 inches (188 cm)

WEIGHT: 270 pounds (122 kg)

HOMETOWN: Warner Robbins, GA

WE ARE THE NATION

Ron Simmons first appeared in WWE as Faarooq, the militant leader of the Nation of Domination. Simmons recruited The Rock, Mark Henry, and others into the controversial faction. He was eventually ousted as the group's leader by The Rock, but the People's Champ still credits Simmons for being a strong influence in his career.

The camera loves Rosa whether in her natural black hair or as a gleaming bleach blonde.

Lots of excited fans wave signs and make frantic efforts to catch a glimpse of their favorite Superstar. Rosa Mendes took it a step further. Her manic enthusiasm earned her an internship with the dominant Diva, Beth Phoenix, and Rosa has called WWE home ever since. After turning the page on "Glamorella" she moved up the ladder to management. She enjoyed a long run handling business matters for Primo and Epico. The beautiful Diva from Costa Rica guided the Colon clan through an impressive reign with the WWE Tag Team Championships. Her goal, however, has not changed from her wide-eyed days of sitting ringside watching The Glamazon. Rosa believes she has what it takes to tangle with the top Divas in WWE. She competed at *WrestleMania 30* for the Divas Championship, and though she did not win, she remains determined to earn that next opportunity.

Rosa's ringside moves are both pleasing to the eye and distracting for competitors.

HEIGHT: 5 feet, 9 inches (175 cm)

FROM: San Jose, Costa Rica

TOTAL ROSA

Rosa watched the first two seasons of *Total Divas* with a keen eye while cameras caught every move of The Bellas, Natalya, and others. For season three, the spicy Latina joined the cast, adding to an already combustible mix of fiery Divas.

RUSEV

Rusev's determined stare looks as if it can burn a hole right through its target.

Short power lifter's trunks display his name and his massive quad muscles.

Rusev competes barefoot, allowing his martial arts kicks to fly with deadly accuracy.

"Rusev Udrea! Rusev Machka!" Under the stern watch of his ravishing ambassador, Rusev enters the ring with one goal in mind: CRUSH! Touted as a supreme example of Russian superiority, he is the ultimate combination of agility, strength, and aggression. Lana reminds the WWE Universe of these attributes each time he competes with her ominous introduction for the Bulgarian Brute. With so many overwhelming displays under his belt, it is hard to dispute Rusev's bold labeling of "super athlete." His true intentions are unclear, as he seems to be somewhat brainwashed. For now, Lana's wish is his command. She seems fixated on showcasing Rusev as a symbol of forceful dominance for his adopted home, mother Russia, where he as been presented a gold star medal and deemed a hero to the Russian Federation. Rusev will unleash his wrath on all who resist his mission to conquer WWE.

HEIGHT: 6 feet (183 cm)

WEIGHT: 305 pounds (138 kg)

HOMETOWN: Russia

SIGNATURE MOVE: The Accolade

INTERNATIONAL THREAT

Rusev's fury is not limited to the United States. His dismantling of all three "Union Jack" members in London, England sent a clear message. He will not waver until the entire globe yields to his superiority.

RYBACK

Ryback brings an explosive combination of raw power and ferocious intensity to the ring. This menacing brute has an appetite for destruction that could never be satisfied. He first turned heads in WWE by dispatching helpless opponents like a wrecking ball to a condemned building with one relentless demand, "Feed me more!" It was clear this insatiable Superstar was ready to wreak havoc on anyone brave enough to stand in his path. Many Superstars have found this out the hard way. Even the unconquerable John Cena has felt Ryback's wrath, at one point getting speared through the *Extreme Rules* set by the massive behemoth. Ryback's rampage through WWE has left no one safe, even backstage. Unable to keep his fury within the ring ropes, he has been seen imposing his brutal will on several unfortunate crew members. While he's not a shining example for WWE's anti-bullying program, the disaster in his wake leaves no denial — Ryback Rules!

> Ryback's intimidating stare is enough to make his opponents shake in their boots.

> Ryback has the appearance of a cyborg bent on human annihilation.

> Ryback's hulking muscles make him a throwback to a time when "big guys" ruled the ring.

HEIGHT: 6 feet, 3 inches (191 cm)

WEIGHT: 291 pounds (132 kg)

HOMETOWN:
Las Vegas, NV

SIGNATURE MOVES:
Shell Shocked

SWINDLED

In 2012, The Human Wrecking Ball was on the verge of crushing CM Punk's WWE Championship reign inside the confines of Hell in a Cell. Only the rogue actions of a corrupt referee prevented Ryback from attaining WWE's grandest prize. Ryback will do whatever it takes to get back to the top, even if it means mixing with unsavory types such as Paul Heyman or Curtis Axel.

SAMI ZAYN

Sami Zayn brings to the ring one of the most eclectic styles ever seen in NXT. A Canadian born Superstar of Syrian descent, Zayn honed his skills in an astounding twenty-nine different countries before taking his skills to Orlando for NXT. His resume reads a lot like a former WWE World Heavyweight Champion, Daniel Bryan—modest size, well-traveled before landing in WWE, unique personality, leaping ability, diverse arsenal of strikes, and devastating submission holds. If Zayn can keep working with the same intensity, maybe a miraculous run to *WrestleMania* can be in his future as well. So far, he is off to a good start. He has asserted himself well against a more experienced WWE Superstar, Cesaro. He also scored a victory in July of 2014 against a former WWE Tag Team Champion, Tyson Kidd. Sami Zayn is ready to meet the next challenge full throttle with a smile on his face.

Sami Zayn competed under a mask in several stops on his journey through independent wrestling. Now, he lets the NXT Universe see his face.

HEIGHT: 6 feet, 1 inch (185 cm)

WEIGHT: 205 pounds (93 kg)

HOMETOWN: Montreal, Quebec

BO-GUS LOSS

Sami Zayn found himself at odds with Bo Dallas in 2013, leading to a personal clash for the *NXT* Championship. Zayn appeared to win when JBL pointed out that Bo's foot was on the rope. The General Manager did not have the same eagle eye when Dallas sent Zayn into an exposed turnbuckle, leading to tough loss for Zayn.

SANTINO MARELLA

Like he and Vladimir Kozlov, Santino's eyebrows were once united, but have since gone their separate ways.

Close encounters with this serpentine sock have been known to leave a man down for the three-count.

Santino Marella does not just dance to the beat of his own drum. He sounds the trombone for his own invisible marching band. One of WWE's most unique Superstars, Santino lived the dream of every fan sitting at ringside in the "Milan Miracle." Answering an open challenge, he emerged from the crowd to win the Intercontinental Championship. Since then, he has spiced up WWE with his own brand of savory Italian seasoning. A hopeless romantic, Santino knows what makes the Divas tick. He did, after all, grow up beside a future Miss *WrestleMania*, his "twin sister" Santina. If it is not the ladies he is charming, it's his giant green cobra, the world's deadliest sock puppet. His humorous quirks are a constant source of entertainment, but Santino's competitive track record is no laughing matter. He has power-walked his way to some of the most sought after titles in WWE over his long, unorthodox career.

HEIGHT: 6 foot, 3 inches (191 cm)
WEIGHT: 233 pounds (106 kg)
HOMETOWN: Calabria, Italy

READY TO RUMBLE

Santino Marella's Italian bravado worked against him at *Royal Rumble 2009*. He charged right into a clothesline from Kane and was eliminated in 1.9 seconds, setting a record. He saved face two years later, nearly creating another miracle before Alberto Del Rio tossed him over the ropes.

SASHA BANKS

Sasha Banks was an original member of the BFFs, and though the team has disbanded, Banks is still one beautiful, fierce female. It all started when someone told her she was not tough or strong enough to make it in NXT. Big mistake. Banks made it her personal mission to prove all skeptics wrong, even if it meant unleashing a darker, malicious side of her personality. She declared herself "The Boss of NXT" and took out her aggression in rivalries with Paige, Emma, Bayley, and others. She and Summer Rae even lured the second-generation Diva Charlotte to their side. Competing as a trio, the BFFs terrorized the NXT Divas division until Charlotte walked out on Banks after a hard fought match. On her own, Banks plans to use her furious style and high-flying arsenal to prove that she never needed help in the first place. All doubters better beware.

Sasha Banks wears a blinged out BOSS chain around her neck to remind everyone who is in charge.

HEIGHT: 5 feet, 5 inches (165 cm)

HOMETOWN: Boston, MA

SIGNATURE MOVE: Bankrupt

FALSE ADMIRER

Sasha Banks once received letters from an anonymous source claiming to be a secret admirer. It was a ruse, however, perpetrated by another Diva, Audrey Marie, who was jealous of her success. Banks earned retribution by defeating Marie in multiple tag team matches.

SAWYER FULTON

Sawyer Fulton is one of few NXT Superstars big enough to pull off a single-strapped top, a look usually reserved for giants.

Sawyer Fulton is one of the youngest Superstars on the NXT roster, but that does not stop him from gunning for the NXT Championship with all the strength in his 285 pound frame. Fulton has never shied away from a fight. As an amateur athlete, he turned to wrestling as a way to channel his aggression. After earning All-American honors in high school he went on to college. While there, he earned NCAA All-American honors twice. Fresh out of college, Fulton is looking to duplicate his success on the next stepping stone, NXT. Working on a farm his whole life, Fulton developed the necessary size and strength to be taken seriously by anyone who stands across from him. In his limited time with NXT, he has taken on all comers with mixed results. He is a green competitor, but hungry. Once he gains a little more experience, look out.

HEIGHT: 6 feet, 8 inches (203 cm)

WEIGHT: 285 pounds (129 kg)

HOMETOWN: Toledo, OH

TOUGH TEST

Sawyer Fulton's lifelong goal was to become a WWE Superstar. When he made his NXT debut it was like a dream come true … until the Wyatt Family ruined the experience for him. He and Travis Tyler did not stand a chance against the terrifying trio who would soon take WWE by storm.

SCOTT DAWSON

Scott Dawson does not worry about sculpting a six-pack for the beach. "Abs never won a fight," he says. "Big plates and big steaks equal big pecs and big checks."

Scott Dawson is NXT's resident roughneck. Whether for sport or for survival, he has spent his whole life fighting. Dawson recalls brawling in the back of a trailer park for money. He has also been a bouncer in some of the toughest neighborhood bars imaginable. Nothing scares Dawson, even the thought of going toe to toe with the toughest young sports-entertainers in the world. He has been criticized for calling himself "Captain Roughneck," but Dawson answers the criticism by working hard and doing what he has to do to get by. To him, that is what being a roughneck is all about. Lately, he has been rumored to be involved with a tag team called The Mechanics, a tribute to blue collar tandems such as The Brainbusters, Hollywood Blondes, and Los Guerreros. Any teams vying for the NXT Tag Team Championships better be leery of these up and coming brawlers.

HEIGHT: 5 feet, 10 inches (178 cm)

WEIGHT: 219 pounds (99 kg)

INSPIRATION

Scott Dawson has been quoted as saying that WWE Hall of Famer Bret "Hit Man" Hart inspires him to strive to be the best he can be. Says Dawson, "He was the absolute best at what he did."

SETH ROLLINS

Two-toned (and if you ask Dean Ambrose and Roman Reigns, two-faced), Seth Rollins has an unmistakable look.

Seth Rollins calls himself The Architect, claiming that The Shield was his vision. If so, Rollins deserves credit for building an indestructible unit then tearing it apart from the inside. Just when the Hounds of Justice were at their strongest, Rollins committed a shocking betrayal, attacking his "brothers" and aligning with Triple H. Was this callous defection "best for business?" Rollins thinks so. He quickly abandoned his Shield gear for a three-piece suit and sleeker ring attire—Authority approved. The WWE Universe believes he sold out. The Aerialist sees it as buying in, and for this one time investment of his soul, he earned an easier path to the coveted Money in the Bank contract. Ambrose and Reigns are not done with him, and his list of enemies is getting longer. Still, with corporate big wigs backing his circus-like acrobatics in the ring, stopping Rollins is easier said than done.

Rollins once balled his fist in unison with The Shield. Now he uses his hand to shake with the corporate powers he once fought against.

HEIGHT: 6 feet, 1 inch (185 cm)
WEIGHT: 217 pounds (98 kg)
HOMETOWN: Davenport, IA
SIGNATURE MOVE: Curb Stomp

THE SHIELD'S LAST STAND

Seth Rollins made jaws drop at *Extreme Rules 2014*. After a wild free-for-all took the combatants outside the ring, The Architect came soaring off the balcony onto his Evolution opponents. The highlight reel moment is surreal in hindsight, as Rollins would defect to The Authority's side in the following weeks.

SGT. SLAUGHTER

Nervous maggots see the reflection of their puke faces in Sgt. Slaughter's shades.

Sgt. Slaughter always walks through the curtain chin first. The rest of him follows seconds later.

Sarge is decked out in camo like a true soldier.

"AT-TEN-HUT!" Today's Superstars and Divas know to stand tall and salute when Sgt. Slaughter marches into a WWE arena. A true legend of the ring, Sarge became an American icon in the 1980s. The former Marine drew the ire of the WWE Universe, browbeating spectators and competitors alike and dismissing them as "maggots." Fans forgave the overbearing drill instructor once he channeled his aggression in defense of the stars and stripes. When Sarge silenced the anti-American diatribes of the Iron Sheik, he achieved full-fledged hero status from sea to shining sea. Sgt. Slaughter's authoritative bark and unmistakable jawline helped put him in the realm of the immortal Hulk Hogan as the most recognizable red, white, and blue protectors. When the American way is challenged, Sgt. Slaughter is sure to return to the ring in all his flag-waving glory to inflict his own brand of justice.

HEIGHT:
6 feet, 6 inches (198 cm)

WEIGHT:
305 pounds (138 kg)

HOMETOWN: Parris Island, SC

SIGNATURE MOVES:
Cobra Clutch

TURNCOAT
Sgt. Slaughter enraged his red-blooded supporters by becoming an Iraqi sympathizer during the first Gulf War. At *WrestleMania VII*, a beating from Hulk Hogan helped snap him out of this malaise. Soon after, forgiving fans accepted his passionate plea, "I want my country back!"

SHAWN MICHAELS

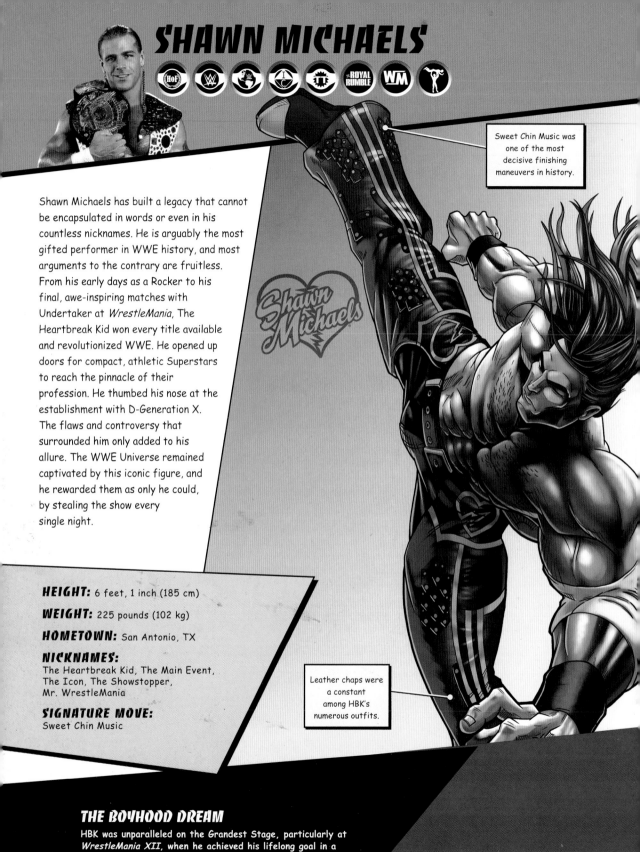

Shawn Michaels has built a legacy that cannot be encapsulated in words or even in his countless nicknames. He is arguably the most gifted performer in WWE history, and most arguments to the contrary are fruitless. From his early days as a Rocker to his final, awe-inspiring matches with Undertaker at *WrestleMania*, The Heartbreak Kid won every title available and revolutionized WWE. He opened up doors for compact, athletic Superstars to reach the pinnacle of their profession. He thumbed his nose at the establishment with D-Generation X. The flaws and controversy that surrounded him only added to his allure. The WWE Universe remained captivated by this iconic figure, and he rewarded them as only he could, by stealing the show every single night.

Sweet Chin Music was one of the most decisive finishing maneuvers in history.

Leather chaps were a constant among HBK's numerous outfits.

HEIGHT: 6 feet, 1 inch (185 cm)

WEIGHT: 225 pounds (102 kg)

HOMETOWN: San Antonio, TX

NICKNAMES:
The Heartbreak Kid, The Main Event, The Icon, The Showstopper, Mr. WrestleMania

SIGNATURE MOVE:
Sweet Chin Music

THE BOYHOOD DREAM
HBK was unparalleled on the Grandest Stage, particularly at *WrestleMania XII*, when he achieved his lifelong goal in a 60-minute Iron Man Match for the WWE Championship.

SHEAMUS

Sheamus descends from a noble bloodline of ancient Celtic Warriors. The first Irish-born WWE Champion in history, Sheamus channels the ferocity of his ancestors in the ring, brutalizing foes with remarkable power. With fiery red hair to match his temper, he relishes the opportunity to fight no matter who stands in his way. Less than a year into his WWE career, Sheamus shocked the world when he sent John Cena crashing through a table to win his first WWE Championship. This pulverizing powerhouse is already one of the most decorated stars of the modern era, and he is just getting started. His punishing offensive style and raw strength give him a leg up on the competition. Sheamus is always a Brogue Kick away from bringing a match to a swift, decisive ending. The Celtic Warrior remains as aggressive as ever and his fighting spirit keeps him determined to take on the next challenge.

Sheamus's unmistakable red hair is accentuated by his milky white skin.

Sheamus's cross pendant harkens back to his Celtic origins. It symbolizes both his warrior strength and ideals.

HEIGHT: 6 feet, 4 inches (193 cm)

WEIGHT: 267 pounds (121 kg)

HOMETOWN: Dublin, Ireland

SIGNATURE MOVES:
Brogue Kick, White Noise, Irish Curse Backbreaker, Cloverleaf

NICKNAMES:
The Celtic Warrior, The Great White

"Laoch" means "warrior" or "hero" in the ancient Gaelic language.

TURNING OVER A NEW CLOVERLEAF

Sheamus's forceful actions earned him a reputation as a bully early in his career. He later saw the error of his ways, and began giving other bullies a taste of their own medicine. Fans took notice and "boos" toward the Irish fella soon turned to cheers.

SIKA

Sika's hair was out of control and made him look even crazier than he was.

Sika is one half of the WWE Hall of Fame tag team The Wild Samoans. Rarely seen without his brother and partner, Afa, Sika is a proud member of the legendary Anoa'i family. The illustrious family includes such stars as The Rock, Rikishi, The Usos, and several others, but The Wild Samoans stand out as the most outlandish of the bunch. Their peculiar grunting and strange dietary habits gave them a psychological edge. Most opponents were no match for their physicality either. The Wild Samoans won three Tag Team Titles while together. Sika pursued a singles career after the team split. He even enlisted the devious Mr. Fuji to help in his cause. He made an appearance at *WrestleMania IV*, but never recaptured the magic he created with his brother. The Wild Samoans eventually reunited, and have worked together for two decades shaping future Superstars with dreams of attaining the same legendary status.

HEIGHT: 6 feet, 2 inches (188 cm)

WEIGHT: 319 pounds (145 kg)

HOMETOWN: The Isle of Samoa

SIGNATURE MOVE:
Samoan Drop, Headbutt

Like a true product of the wild, Sika competed barefoot.

PROVING GROUND

The Wild Samoan Training center has a laundry list of prominent alumni including Batista, Billy Kidman, Umaga, and more. The legacy of Sika and Afa lives on through younger members of the Anoa'i family and through their successful graduates.

SIMON GOTCH

Simon Gotch flaunts his manliness by performing one-arm pushups while subduing his opponents.

Gotch's handlebar mustache puts the "villain" in Vaudevillian.

Simon Gotch does not wear kneepads like most Superstars. They were probably not invented in the early 20th century.

Simon Gotch brings a unique style to NXT that harkens back to the earliest days of sports-entertainment. Whether an ancestral link exists between this "Gentleman Bruiser" and Frank Gotch, one of the first World Heavyweight Champions of the early 1900s, is unknown. Even an early pioneer like Frank Gotch might call Simon a throwback if he were still alive today. He touts an undefeated record in "matches versus bears" and has formed a vaudeville inspired team with fellow eccentric, Aiden English. Some might consider Gotch peculiar. Gotch considers himself "quite manly." He is known for performing feats of strength in the ring that are fit for the circus. Now that he has transitioned from bears to NXT's top Superstars, this "Steam-Powered Madman" is eager to take his old school flavor to the forefront of NXT. With Aiden English aiding his cause, this Vaudevillian is always ready for a scrum.

HEIGHT: 6 feet, 1 inch (185 cm)

WEIGHT: 221 pounds (100 kg)

HOMETOWN: Arkham, MA

SIGNATURE MOVES:
Gentleman's Clutch

OPENING ACT
The NXT Universe did not know what to expect from The Vaudevillians when they debuted on June 19, 2014. William Regal joked that he wanted to see a chimpanzee on a bicycle. What he did see was this new team dominate Angelo Dawkins and Travis Tyler in their first match.

SIN CARA

Unlike other luchadors, Sin Cara's mask has no opening for his mouth, keeping his identity completely hidden.

Before taking flight in WWE, Sin Cara was a household name in his home country of Mexico. The acclaimed lucha libre star took his highflying spectacle to the big stage in 2011. The mesmerizing masked man, whose name literally means "without face," has been one of WWE's most captivating performers ever since. When Sin Cara competes the arena takes on a special glow, as if WWE has shifted into a parallel universe where gravity no longer exists. Sin Cara's greatest challenge has come from a black-masked imposter of himself, Sin Cara (Negro). After a pulse pounding series of matches contested mostly through the air, the original Sin Cara proved to be the one and only. Do not expect any verbose, on camera interviews from Sin Cara. The WWE Universe knows when that mystifying glow engulfs the ring, his aerial attack will do all the talking he needs.

Sin Cara covers his arms with tight fitting sleeves that match his mask.

Sin Cara recently abandoned his traditional gold and powder blue and has been seen sporting the red, green, and white of his native Mexico.

HEIGHT: 5 feet, 7 inches (170 cm)
WEIGHT: 180 pounds (82 kg)
HOMETOWN: Mexico City, Mexico

FACELESS ALLIANCE

Sin Cara found an ally in WWE's original masked avenger, Rey Mysterio, in 2012. Two of Mexico's greatest exports teamed up to take on the best tag teams in WWE. Though they never reached the Tag Team Titles, they did score victories over Team Hell No, The Prime Time Players, and others.

STARDUST

When gazing up into the brightest constellations in the night sky, you might notice something missing. That shining star you are looking for has descended into a WWE ring as the reborn younger brother of Goldust. Stardust is an intergalactic wunderkind. He has arrived seeking more from the earth than what meets his crimson eyes. He derives strength from his own stellar psyche all the way to the furthest reaches of the galaxy. He channels this strength into his relentless quest for a greater truth. To the casual observer he is a younger, more nimble version of his bizarre brother, but that description only scratches the surface of Stardust. There is still much to learn about this gold and black enigma. What is his ultimate mission? Does he even know? How long is he here to stay? Only time will tell. For now, the truth is out there ... and so is Stardust.

> Stardust peers through a solitary black star over a gilded background with his blazing red eyes.

> Stardust's tight fitting suit echoes his brother's colors with more star patterns for his own personal flair.

> Each of Stardust's gloves is adorned with half a star, which forms an intergalactic symmetry when he joins them together.

HEIGHT: 6 feet, 2 inches (188 cm)

WEIGHT: 220 pounds (100 kg)

HOMETOWN: Marietta, GA

TRUE FORM

Since his transformation, Stardust has been overflowing with confidence, leading many to wonder if this was really his true self all along. Though he seeks more than just wins, wins are a good first step to enlightenment. His newfound identity has produced the intended result so far.

STEPHANIE MCMAHON

A decisive leader, Stephanie possesses in-depth knowledge of all facets of the business.

Stephanie McMahon was born WWE royalty. Growing up, her father's pioneering ways inspired her to share his passion for sports-entertainment. As Mr. McMahon built WWE into a global empire, he passed along his wisdom and drive to his only daughter. Today, Stephanie is a pioneer herself, defying the notion that WWE is a "man's world." Stephanie shatters this stereotype in and out of the ring. By day, she champions executive strategies at WWE headquarters. By night, she makes hardened, muscle-bound tough guys cry on national television. Stephanie is determined to blaze her own trail as a WWE monarch. She works around the clock laying the groundwork for the next era of WWE, keeping a close eye on today's Superstars. Her actions may not always be popular, but are always "Best for Business."

Stephanie keeps in tiptop shape, and is not afraid to mix it up in the ring.

HOMETOWN: Greenwich, CT

POSITION: Chief Brand Officer

CAREER HIGHLIGHTS:
Before The Authority usurped absolute power in WWE, Stephanie headed up both *Raw* and *SmackDown* as General Manager. She also struck a coup against her father by forming the WCW/ECW Alliance with her brother, Shane.

HISTORY COMES FULL CIRCLE
Years ago, Stephanie spurned daddy dearest and aligned with Triple H, ushering in the McMahon-Helmsley era. Today, she and the King of Kings form the ultimate power couple. Known as The Authority, they impose their executive will on the entire WWE Universe.

STING

This is Sting. Once a vibrant, bleach-blonde warrior with a battle cry as jarring as his neon face paint, the ongoing clash between good and evil swept dark shadows over his soul. "The Franchise of WCW" transformed to a brooding, ghostly symbol, lurking in the rafters like a haunting apparition. Although he fell silent, his actions spoke volumes. One menacing point of his black bat was worth a thousand words. Sting never relinquished his status as the lone symbol of an era. He captivated sports-entertainment fans with stone-faced determination until the lights blinked out on *WCW Nitro* in 2001. Having collected seven World Titles and countless accolades in his career, Sting is widely regarded as the greatest Superstar in WCW history and the greatest Superstar never to grace a WWE ring. Still, on nights with an eerie chill in the air, the WWE Superstars cannot help but gaze up into the rafters, and wonder ...

Whether neon or pale white with ghoulish designs, Sting's face was the face of WCW.

Sting's flowing black trench coat blends into the noir landscape from which he descends.

Sting's black bat was used more for identifying his next target than striking his opponents.

HEIGHT: 6 feet, 2 inches (188 cm)

WEIGHT: 250 pounds (113 kg)

HOMETOWN: Venice Beach, CA

SIGNATURE MOVES: Scorpion Death Lock, Stinger Splash, Scorpion Death Drop

A RIVALRY WITH FLAIR

Sting proved his mettle at the inaugural *Clash of the Champions* in a grueling, 45-minute draw with "Nature Boy" Ric Flair. The two fabled Superstars would go on to square off at the 1990 *Great American Bash* as well as the first and last episodes of *Monday Nitro*.

STONE COLD STEVE AUSTIN

Austin 3:16

Stone Cold Steve Austin is the undeniable face of WWE's Attitude Era. Brash, defiant, and always ready to raise Hell, Austin could care less who stood in his path. From the Chairman of WWE, to The Rock, and even to boxing legend Mike Tyson, Stone Cold just saw a mud hole begging to be stomped and walked dry. When he gave Mr. McMahon a certain single-digit salute and flattened him with his patented Stunner, the employed public reveled in this fantasy, and Austin became a working class hero. For several years, Stone Cold produced countless iconic moments and accolades on his way to the WWE Hall of Fame. Though he is now retired, there is no predicting when the sound of shattered glass will echo through the arena, signaling mayhem for all who stand in his way.

Stone Cold's signature black vest was adorned with a skull emblem and the letters 3:16.

Austin was never flashy, choosing instead to wear plain black and let his actions gain him attention.

HEIGHT: 6 feet, 2 inches (188 cm)

WEIGHT: 252 pounds (114 kg)

HOMETOWN: Victoria, TX

SIGNATURE MOVE:
Stone Cold Stunner

A LEGEND IS BORN

Stone Cold's cutting remarks at the 1996 *King of the Ring* tournament gave birth to the "Austin 3:16" phenomenon. Within weeks, virtually every WWE fan owned an "Austin 3:16" t-shirt.

SUMMER RAE

They say blondes have more fun, and Summer Rae is living it up so far in her young career.

Summer Rae is always dressed to the nines, though her beauty and dance moves get a unanimous ten.

Her name sounds innocent enough, but do not underestimate the steamy Summer Rae. She claims partial responsibility for one of the most illustrious debuts in history. When Fandango fox-trotted his way onto the scene in 2013, he instantly scored a win on the Grandest Stage at *WrestleMania 29* on the way to a praiseworthy rookie year. Summer Rae influenced these early bouts without laying a hand on anyone. Her natural ability to deviate the eyes of opponents was just the X factor needed for the tangoing twosome to start their careers on the right foot. Unfortunately, Fandango skipped dancing school the day they taught loyalty, and he dumped Summer at the first sign of adversity. With her boogying beau out of the picture, Summer is ready to move on to bigger and better things. She hardly took an interlude before setting her sights on the best competition in the Divas division.

HEIGHT: 5 feet, 10 inches (178 cm)

HOMETOWN: Raleigh, NC

Summer Rae's enchanting long legs are reminiscent of Stacey Keibler.

SYLVESTER LEFORT

Sylvester LeFort is one half of The Legionnaires, a NXT tag team full of French blood and swagger. Together with Marcus Louis, he is a thorn in the side of Colin Cassady, Enzo Amore, and anyone else who finds his arrogance as easy to swallow as a jagged, bitter pill. Before finding a kindred spirit in Louis, LeFort ran with another anti-American villain, Rusev. He also competed in singles action and worked as a manager. LeFort is a confident competitor. He believes he can take down anyone who steps in the ring with him, saying, "I am not a big guy, but I will do some big things." With this kind of tenacity, it would not shock anyone to see LeFort flying a French flag on *Monday Night Raw* in the near future. He already views himself as a worldwide attraction, and is well on his way to proving himself right.

LeFort peers out at the NXT audience through shades that only he can afford.

HEIGHT: 5 feet, 11 inches (180 cm)

WEIGHT: 190 pounds (86 kg)

HOMETOWN: Nice, France

ENTREPRENUER

. Sylvester LeFort was first seen by the NXT Universe touting himself as a wealthy entrepreneur. His first management venture was managing the southern bred team of Garrett Dylan and Scott Dawson.

TAMINA SNUKA

Tamina looks mean in her trademark black leather.

Tamina is not your typical Barbie doll. She has the beauty to steal your attention and the brawn to steal your lunch money.

Tamina Snuka is not your typical Diva. Just over thirty years ago, her Hall of Fame father, Jimmy Snuka, was perched 15 feet high atop a Steel Cage, inspiring a generation. Now, the next generation in the Snuka bloodline carries the Superfly's legacy. Tamina leaps from the top turnbuckle with the same uninhibited zeal as her dear old dad. She also works an intimidation factor unmatched by her Diva contemporaries.

Tamina's deadpan stare to the opposite corner of the ring is enough for the psychological edge. Once things get physical, matching the strength of this brawny babe is a near exercise in futility. For the better part of a year, she put her imposing traits to use as the enforcer for Divas Champion AJ Lee. Tamina does not need any backup herself, though. She knows she is championship material and is always a Splash away from reaching her goal.

HEIGHT: 5 feet, 9 inches (175 cm)
HOMETOWN: Pacific Islands
SIGNATURE MOVES:
Superfly Splash

DUALING DYNASTIES
Tamina began her career as part of a multi-generational trio with the sons of WWE Legend Rikishi, The Usos. The group formed a natural rivalry with Canadian counterparts, the Hart Dynasty. The allied sectors traded hard-fought victories. Tamina and Natalya remain adversaries in the Diva's division today.

181

TERRY FUNK

Raised on sports-entertainment in Amarillo, Texas, by his legendary father, Dory Funk Sr., Terry Funk kept the family tradition going. He took the Double Cross Ranch style around the country, the world, and later on, to the extreme. Though he has plied his craft for five decades, three fateful years in ECW would come to define him. After joining up with the budding hardcore promotion, the tough Texan became surrounded by barbed wire, thumbtacks, branding irons, and anything else that inflicts unfathomable anguish. He felt right at home. The "middle aged and crazy" brawler was worshipped by the hardcore faithful. His matches against counter-culture renegades such as Cactus Jack and Tommy Dreamer were not for the faint of heart. However, the rabid, cult-like ECW fan base loved every minute. Funk made sporadic appearances in WWE throughout his career, and is enshrined with his brother, Dory Jr., in the Hall of Fame.

At curtain stops in his career, Funk wore a cowboy hat and played up his roots as a Texas outlaw.

Terry Funk's striped trunks were a signature, as was the sight of Funk dishing out and absorbing massive amounts of punishment.

HEIGHT: 6 feet, 1 inch (185 cm)

WEIGHT: 247 pounds (112 kg)

HOMETOWN: Amarillo, TX

SIGNATURE MOVE:
Spinning Toe Hold

CHAIN SAW CHARLIE

Terry Funk had a memorable run in WWE as Chainsaw Charlie. The well-travelled bruiser was welcome by everyone in WWE—everyone but the New Age Outlaws. The brash young duo hurled Funk and Cactus Jack off the side of the cage in a dumpster. True to form, Funk emerged and was 100% in no time.

THEODORE LONG

Teddy possesses unparalleled knowledge of sports-entertainment.

Teddy Long has seen it all in sports-entertainment. Revered today as the longest tenured General Manager in *SmackDown* history, Long paid his dues before attaining that position in 2004. In a lifetime of bouncing from arena to arena, Teddy has worked every job from referee to manager to floor sweeper. It should come as no surprise that his leadership on the blue brand was punctuated by a keen eye for entertainment, conviction in his decision-making, and an unmatched respect for the business. Despite his small stature, Long tolerated zero guff from the burliest bruisers on the roster. Mr. McMahon respects this kind of gumption, which explains Teddy's impressive staying power in WWE. He has since accepted lessor roles under the likes of John Laurinaitis, Booker T, and Vickie Guerrero, but Long still brings the same enthusiastic strut to work every day, ready for the next challenge.

Teddy's wide assortment of suits always gives him the style of a true playa'.

HEIGHT: 5 feet, 7 inches (170 cm)

WEIGHT: 173 pounds (78 kg)

HOMETOWN: Atlanta, GA

BATTLE OF THE BRANDS

Superstars in WWE once competed exclusively on either *Raw* or *SmackDown*, and in 2005, the two separate brands were at odds. Teddy Long was fed up with his camp being referred to as the "B show." He took matters in his own hands and challenged *Raw* GM Eric Bischoff at *Survivor Series*. With a little help from The Boogeyman, he dropped his counterpart for a 1-2-3.

THE MIZ

A torrent of verbal barbs lies just behind Miz's sly expression.

His "faux hawk" days may be over, but Miz still has his red carpet style.

The Miz ditched his baggy shorts for more traditional ring trunks once he launched his solo career.

IM AWESOME

If you think he is obnoxious… you are probably right. However, you would be, too, if you were as awesome as The Miz. When this former *Real World* star made it to the finals of WWE's *Tough Enough* series, nobody took him seriously. They do now. The Miz overcame the reality TV stigma. A decade later, he is still living the dream of every kid who grew up impersonating WWE Superstars in the mirror. He spends his Monday nights armed with a microphone, ready to ask the tough questions and, of course, toot his own horn. As the saying goes, it's not bragging if you back it up, and Miz has the hardware to match his motor mouth. He is one of seven men in history to walk into *WrestleMania* as WWE Champion and retain the gold. The Miz remains one of the most must-see attractions in WWE. Really.

HEIGHT: 6 feet, 2 inches (188 cm)

WEIGHT: 220 pounds (100 kg)

HOMETOWN: Cleveland, OH

SIGNATURE MOVES: Skull-crushing Finale, Figure-Four Leglock

THE AWESOME HALF

The Miz shines on his own, but also makes a tremendous tag team partner. He and John Morrison formed a groundbreaking team that dominated the ring and the web with their entertaining internet show, *The Dirt Sheet*. R-Truth and Big Show have also seen success teaming with The Awesome One.

THE ROCK

The People's Eyebrow. When raised, know your role and shut your mouth.

Tattoos proudly display The Rock's Samoan heritage.

The Rock has greatness coded into his DNA. Descending from a legendary sports entertainment family, Dwayne Johnson has shattered his own lofty expectations by becoming the most electrifying man in all of entertainment. He gained notoriety with the villainous Nation of Domination, but his undying charisma quickly earned him millions (and millions) of passionate supporters. He became "The People's Champ" and never looked back. With the WWE Universe in the palm of his hand every step of the way, The Rock has truly done it all. He has stood victorious in *WrestleMania* main events, won every major championship and even crossed over to the silver screen to conquer the bright lights of Hollywood. Whether strutting down the red carpet or a WWE entrance ramp, "The Great One" is always ready to lay the smackdown at a moment's notice.

HEIGHT: 6 feet 5 inches (196 cm)

WEIGHT: 260 pounds (118 kg)

HOMETOWN: Miami, FL

SIGNATURE MOVES:
Rock Bottom, People's Elbow

The Rock electrifies the crowd by dropping the People's Elbow on his opponents.

JUST BROUGHT IT
The Rock's miraculous WWE comeback came full circle at *Royal Rumble* 2013 when he did exactly what he promised to do. He toppled CM Punk to reclaim the WWE Championship for the first time in ten years.

TITO SANTANA

Arriba! Tito Santana put together a unique and impressive career with WWE. Not only was he the man to break Don Muraco's year-long stranglehold on the Intercontinental Championship, he became the first Mexican-American Superstar to hold the illustrious title. He was also a matador long before Los Matadores tugged on their first *traje de luces*. Tito Santana is a true original. It is appropriate that he claims the distinction of being the first ever winner of a *WrestleMania* match, forcing The Executioner to submit in the opener of the first Show of Shows. Mr. McMahon picked Santana's match to open the show, trusting that the determined competitor would get the crowd brimming with excitement, and did he ever! Santana was always in the hunt for championship gold in both singles and tag team competition. For his longevity and versatility, he is a deserved member of the WWE Hall of Fame.

> Tito Santana often threw a triumphant fist in the air to lead the crowd in shouting "Arriba!"

> Tito Santana finished opponents by launching his entire body and connecting with a forearm blow to the noggin.

HEIGHT: 6 feet, 2 inches (188 cm)
WEIGHT: 234 pounds (106 kg)
HOMETOWN: Tocula, Mexico
SIGNATURE MOVE: Flying Forearm

WRESTLEMANIA REGULAR

Tito Santana was a participant in the first nine *WrestleMania* events. The only other man who could say that? Hulk Hogan. As a Superstar, any time your name is mentioned alongside the Hulkster you must have done something right!

TITUS O'NEIL

Titus gets riled up by giving the crowd a loud, aggressive bark.

Titus O'Neil's strength and wing span allow him to perform his signature move with devastating force.

Titus O'Neil is a perfect fit for the rough-and-tumble world of WWE. A towering athletic specimen, Titus used his beast-like frame to brutalize opposing quarterbacks in the Southeastern Conference and, later, the NFL. He claims to have come to WWE looking to be "the man." When his partnership with fellow NXT graduate Darren Young began to hold him back, he wasted no time severing ties emphatically. After a string of losses, he snapped and battered his former friend. Whether Titus made the right decision is yet to be seen. As the Prime Time Players, he and Young showed enormous potential. They may not have made "Millions of Dollars," but fans were drawn to their enthusiasm for the ring. Now with a surly attitude and a nastiness to his game, the WWE Universe will be watching O'Neil with great curiosity, waiting to see if he proves to be the "Real Deal."

HEIGHT: 6 feet, 6 inches (198 cm)

WEIGHT: 270 pounds (122 kg)

HOMETOWN: Live Oak, FL

SIGNATURE MOVES:
Clash of the Titus

PRIME TIME SHOWDOWN

Titus' former partner, Darren Young, did not go away quietly. The jilted "Mr. No Days Off" jumped him on *SmackDown* the week after their falling out, ensuring that the rivalry would continue. Titus gained bragging rights in the ongoing beef when he defeated Darren at *Elimination Chamber 2014.*

TRIPLE H

> Despite a new buzz cut befitting an executive, Triple H is still every bit as dangerous.

Triple H has been called The Game, The Cerebral Assassin, and the King of Kings. Now, WWE Superstars have a new name for him: boss. After a peerless in-ring career that earned him demigod status across the WWE landscape, Triple H's kingdom has finally come. Perched atop the WWE empire alongside WWE's queen bee, Stephanie McMahon, his word is the letter of the law. Triple H rules with the same iron fist that propelled him to thirteen World Championships. Knowing the weight of WWE's future rests firmly on his shoulders, Triple H will stop at nothing to do what is "Best for Business." If that means shedding his suit and settling matters in the ring, then so be it. He has not lost a step between the ropes.

> The Game's sledgehammer is always within arm's reach when extreme measures are needed.

HEIGHT: 6 feet, 4 inches (193 cm)

WEIGHT: 255 pounds (116 kg)

HOMETOWN: Greenwich, CT

POSITION:
Chief Operating Officer

SIGNATURE MOVE:
Pedigree

BORN TO LEAD

Triple H and best friend, Shawn Michaels, sparked the revolutionary Attitude Era as cofounders of D-Generation X. Later, The Game ignited Randy Orton and Batista's careers with Evolution. Today, he shepherds tomorrow's Superstars from his state-of-the-art WWE Performance Center in Orlando, Florida.

TRISH STRATUS

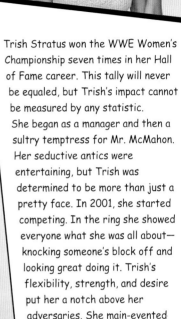

Trish Stratus won her seventh Women's Championship in her final match. Retiring as champion was a deserved honor.

The sight of Trish in her ring gear drew countless marriage proposals from certain segments of the audience.

Trish Stratus won the WWE Women's Championship seven times in her Hall of Fame career. This tally will never be equaled, but Trish's impact cannot be measured by any statistic.

She began as a manager and then a sultry temptress for Mr. McMahon. Her seductive antics were entertaining, but Trish was determined to be more than just a pretty face. In 2001, she started competing. In the ring she showed everyone what she was all about—knocking someone's block off and looking great doing it. Trish's flexibility, strength, and desire put her a notch above her adversaries. She main-evented *Monday Night Raw* with her archrival, Lita, and dazzled onlookers while delivering some Stratusfaction. Today, when the women of WWE lace up in pursuit of becoming a Divas Champion, they are aspiring to become the next Trish Stratus. She is the walking definition of everything that makes a WWE Diva.

HEIGHT:
5 feet, 5 inches (165 cm)

HOMETOWN: Toronto, Ontario

SIGNATURE MOVE:
Stratusfaction

STILL TOUGH ENOUGH

Trish Stratus returned to serve as a trainer for the rebooted *Tough Enough* series in 2011. But first, she decided to prove that after five years away, she still had it. She teamed with John Morrison and Nicole "Snooki" Polizzi and gave Lay-Cool a lesson in humility.

TROY MCCLAIN

Troy McClain uses a hands-free microphone to deliver his motivational pep talks to the NXT Universe.

Troy McClain excelled in three different sports in high school on the way to becoming an NCAA Division 1 athlete. Now that he is making his way in WWE's proving ground, the self-professed "work horse" has discovered his outspoken side. He has promised to outwork the entire NXT roster on the way to becoming its champion. In his first year in NXT, McClain spent most of his time teaming with Travis Tyler. The duo took on all comers in the NXT tag team division. Though they competed with determination, they did not enjoy much time in the winners' circle. McClain has tried his hand in singles competition as well, impressing the NXT Universe with his aggressive, fearless style. His career is just getting started, and if he continues to be a "work horse," the best is yet to come from this promising youngster.

HEIGHT: 6 feet, 3 inches (191 cm)

WEIGHT: 230 pounds (104 kg)

HOMETOWN: Amboy, IL

PARTNERS' CLASH

Troy McClain and Travis Tyler teamed together for the better part of a year. However, in December of 2013 they found themselves competing against each other in a one-on-one match. McClain scored the victory, earning the first

TYE DILLINGER

Tye Dillinger is a skilled tactician with enough talent and guile to feel confident about his quest to win gold in NXT and WWE. Not colorful or flashy, Dillinger doesn't feel the need to be too over-the-top to get noticed. He is understated, but his pointed remarks and smooth style in the ring have the NXT Universe paying attention. Dillinger's boldest comment thus far has been, "There are guys that are bigger than me, stronger than me, and faster than me. However, if they want to be considered the best here in NXT, they just need to be better than Tye Dillinger. I wish them all a great deal of luck." Having no shortage of confidence to match his skill, it is no wonder that Jason Jordan agreed to pair up with Dillinger to compete for the NXT Tag Team Championships.

Dillinger keeps his demeanor at an even keel but can dial up the intensity when it matters.

HEIGHT: 6 feet, 3 inches (191 cm)

WEIGHT: 223 pounds (101 kg)

HOMETOWN: Niagara Falls, Canada

TAG TEAM TRIUMPHS

Dillinger and Jordan went on quite a roll in tag team competition in 2014. The hardworking pair claimed victories over Aiden English and Simon Gotch, Bare Corbin and Sawyer Fulton, and others.

TYLER BREEZE

Breeze claims to use a mixture of coconut, fish oil, and lip balm to maintain the appropriate plumpness of his lips.

Breeze's phone is never out of reach, even in the ring. The arrogant youngster has been known to delay his matches for the sake of snapping another candid likeness.

Don't hate him because he is gorgeous. Of all the fresh faces getting their start in NXT, Tyler Breeze is the prettiest, at least in his own mind. "Prince Pretty" first took his self-absorbed strut down the NXT ramp in July 2013. Puckering up for a "selfie" in an outfit that would make a peacock look modest, it is surprising that Breeze would put his face in harm's way competing in the ring rather than strike a pose on a runway somewhere. All preening and primping aside, however, Breeze's tenacious in-ring style is just as worthy of a photo op as his freshly waxed eyebrows. His face may not feature a bad side, but his personality does. Breeze can abandon the rulebook to steal a victory and have no problem looking in the mirror. With a smile full of pearly whites and not a hair out of place, how could he?

A mismatched outfit is what Breeze calls a "deal-breaker." Breeze coordinates his fur with his gem-colored tights for a look that screams "Superstar." His coat also provides heat therapy for his tanned muscles.

HEIGHT: 6 feet (183 cm)

WEIGHT: 206 pounds (93 kg)

HOMETOWN: Seasonal residences

SIGNATURE MOVE: Beauty Shot

#SELFIE

Tyler Breeze represented a glaring omission in the music video for the hit song "#SELFIE" by The Chainsmokers. Then a social media onslaught became so overwhelming the band added his milkweed-oiled mug to an updated version that went viral. Breeze also stars in his own video "MMMGorgeous."

TYSON KIDD

Tyson Kidd trained in a dungeon to get to where he is today. No one else in WWE will ever be able to say that again. Long before the WWE Performance Center, the Hart Family Dungeon churned out battle tested Superstars like a factory assembly line. Its lineage of stars includes Superstar Billy Graham, Brian Pillman, and of course, its namesake family: The Harts. As the last graduate from Calgary's illustrious proving ground, Tyson Kidd carries an enormous burden on his shoulders. If he is feeling any pressure, you wouldn't know it. After a successful stint in pink and black with David Hart Smith and Natalya, Kidd has struck out on his own. As a singles star, he still displays impeccable ring savvy and tireless work ethic: the Hart signature. The dungeon might have closed its doors, but its lessons live on, forever instilled in the heart of Tyson Kidd.

HEIGHT: 5 feet, 10 inches (178 cm)

WEIGHT: 195 pounds (88 kg)

HOMETOWN: Calgary, Alberta, Canada

SIGNATURE MOVES:
Sharpshooter

A heart on Kidd's trunks is a subtle nod to his upbringing and The Hart Dynasty

TOTAL TYSON

Tyson Kidd has always been like family to the Harts. Now he is official. Tyson did not just learn wristlocks and takedowns in Calgary. He also met his future wife, WWE Diva Natalya. Natalya is the niece of Bret "Hit Man" Hart and Owen Hart. The two talented stars tied the knot on the hit show, *Total Divas*.

ULTIMATE WARRIOR

Warrior's face paint followed a signature pattern with limitless color combinations.

With manic intensity never-before seen or equaled since, Ultimate Warrior is one of WWE's greatest enigmas. Hailing from Parts Unknown, his vibrant neon face paint, superhero physique, and mystifying interviews captivated the WWE Universe. Warrior charged to the ring as if shot out of a cannon while his blistering entrance music shook the rafters. After violently shaking the ring ropes, he devastated opponents with that same aggression. This dominance propelled him to a historic reign with the richest prize in entertainment, the WWE Championship. Though he mysteriously vanished as quickly as his career skyrocketed, he left a lasting impact in WWE. In 2014, this legendary powerhouse was honored with induction into the WWE Hall of Fame.

Warrior's trunks varied in color but always matched his ensemble.

Matching tassels punctuated his larger-than-life appearance.

HEIGHT: 6 feet, 2 inches (188 cm)

WEIGHT: 280 pounds (127 kg)

HOMETOWN: Parts Unknown

SIGNATURE MOVE:
Gorilla Press Slam

THE ULTIMATE CHALLENGE

Ultimate Warrior's defining moment came at *WrestleMania VI*. In what was dubbed "The Ultimate Challenge," Warrior defeated the immortal Hulk Hogan, becoming the first Superstar to hold the WWE Championship and Intercontinental Championships simultaneously.

UNDERTAKER

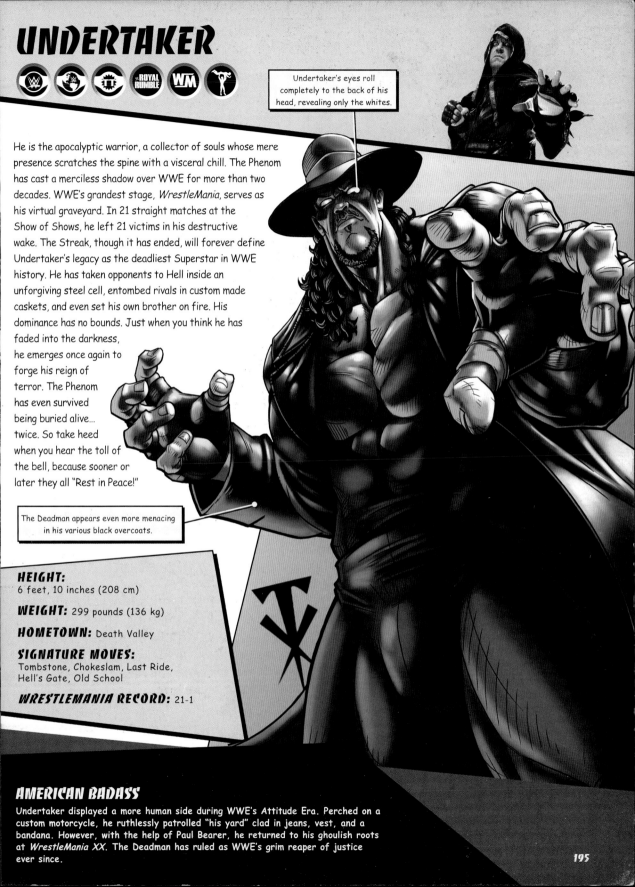

Undertaker's eyes roll completely to the back of his head, revealing only the whites.

He is the apocalyptic warrior, a collector of souls whose mere presence scratches the spine with a visceral chill. The Phenom has cast a merciless shadow over WWE for more than two decades. WWE's grandest stage, *WrestleMania*, serves as his virtual graveyard. In 21 straight matches at the Show of Shows, he left 21 victims in his destructive wake. The Streak, though it has ended, will forever define Undertaker's legacy as the deadliest Superstar in WWE history. He has taken opponents to Hell inside an unforgiving steel cell, entombed rivals in custom made caskets, and even set his own brother on fire. His dominance has no bounds. Just when you think he has faded into the darkness, he emerges once again to forge his reign of terror. The Phenom has even survived being buried alive... twice. So take heed when you hear the toll of the bell, because sooner or later they all "Rest in Peace!"

The Deadman appears even more menacing in his various black overcoats.

HEIGHT:
6 feet, 10 inches (208 cm)

WEIGHT: 299 pounds (136 kg)

HOMETOWN: Death Valley

SIGNATURE MOVES:
Tombstone, Chokeslam, Last Ride, Hell's Gate, Old School

WRESTLEMANIA RECORD: 21-1

AMERICAN BADASS

Undertaker displayed a more human side during WWE's Attitude Era. Perched on a custom motorcycle, he ruthlessly patrolled "his yard" clad in jeans, vest, and a bandana. However, with the help of Paul Bearer, he returned to his ghoulish roots at *WrestleMania XX*. The Deadman has ruled as WWE's grim reaper of justice ever since.

VADER

Vader's trademark red mask did not conceal much of his face, but still made him look more frightening than he already was.

If the Rocky Mountains turned red and black and stomped toward the nearest ring, it would resemble "Vader time." Better known for the devastation he inflicted through Japan and WCW, Vader splashed into WWE in 1996. The masked Mastodon immediately made the earth shake beneath his feet with a performance that earned him a WWE Championship Match at *SummerSlam*. Whether under the guidance of Jim Cornette or Paul Bearer, the human boulder showed the same brutality that earned him international notoriety. He also showcased the same pulverizing maneuvers, which required a surprising agility before gravity did its job. "The Man They Call Vader" vanished from WWE as quickly as he arrived. He never equaled the success he had while working for WWE's competition. Still, his lasting legacy remains. Fans will always remember, "It's time. It's time. It's Vader time," as the eternal warning that an angry Mastodon is on the loose.

The last thing many opponents saw before getting their bones squished was "VADER TIME" printed in a threatening black and red.

HEIGHT: 6 feet, 5 inches (196 cm)

WEIGHT: 450 pounds (204 kg)

HOMETOWN: The Rocky Mountains

SIGNATURE MOVE:
Vader Bomb, Vadersault

VADER TIME, ANY TIME

No one can predict when Vader will strike next. He returned in 2005 to work enforcements for Jonathan Coachman alongside Goldust at *Taboo Tuesday*. Seven years later on *Raw's* 1000th episode, Vader brought the crowd to their collective feet by silencing the "One Man Band" Heath Slater. He still keeps his mask handy in case duty calls.

VERONICA LANE

Veronica Lane is a former beauty queen and model with a burgeoning career as a NXT Diva. The NXT Universe got their first glimpse at her stunning good looks in October 2013. The former Miss Lubbock Texas Teen and runner up for Miss Texas Teen USA embraced her history of pageantry as part of her persona. However, she was not shy about jumping between NXT's yellow ropes and proving she belonged among her new peers who aspire to be future WWE Superstars. Miss Lane has since resurfaced as a ring announcer and backstage interviewer. Veronica's goal is to one day wave to an appreciative crowd with the NXT Women's Championship slung over her shoulder where her sash used to be. It is difficult to predict if she will get there, but at the young age of 23 with nothing but the future ahead, anything is possible for this bright young Diva.

Veronica Lane was first seen on NXT showcasing her success as a beauty queen by wearing a tiara and sash.

Veronica Lane's smile lit up several beauty pageants as a youth and now lights up the NXT arena at Full Sail University.

HEIGHT: 5 feet, 7 inches (170 cm)

HOMETOWN: Waco, TX

FIGHTING BACK

Veronica Lane suffered her first setback in the summer of 2014 when she sustained an injury. However, a peek inside the WWE Performance Center showed a spunky Lane as upbeat as ever, hard at work to get back in the ring.

VICKIE GUERRERO

Excuse me!!! Vickie Guerrero's screeching howl shattered windows in arenas across the globe as she connived her way to power in WWE. No matter how loud fans tried to drown out her voice with boos, she always turned up the dial to a higher decibel level. Having wielded authoritative power over both *Raw* and *SmackDown*, Vickie was one of the most influential power brokers of all time. Her judgment earned its share of criticism, both from Superstar rosters and the governing powers at WWE Headquarters. She also played a dangerous round of hokey pokey with the lines of professionalism, having questionable relationships with stars such as Edge and Dolph Ziggler. Still, Vickie clawed her way up WWE's decision-making totem pole. Though fired by Stephanie McMahon, Vickie left her mark by doing whatever it took to suceed even if it meant lying, cheating, or stealing. Her late husband Eddie would smile.

Vickie had an uncanny tendency to have pies, cakes, and other confectionary items smashed in her face.

Vickie's ear-piercing voice may have been annoying, but when she spoke, Superstars listened!

Vickie does not take any more pot shots for her appearance. She transformed her image to attain full-fledged "cougar" status.

HEIGHT: 5 feet, 4 inches (163 cm)

HOMETOWN: El Paso, TX

SIGNATURE MOVE:
Cougar Splash

POSITIONS HELD: *Raw* General Manager, *SmackDown* General Manager, *Raw* Managing Supervisor, Official Consultant to *SmackDown*

CATCHPHRASE: "Excuse me!!!"

FEELING FROGGY

Vickie Guerrero's bias toward Lay-Cool and other devious Divas earned her a trip to the ring at *WrestleMania XXVI*. In a multi-Diva clash, Vickie stole the show by stealing a page from a familiar playbook. After shimmying up to the top rope, she landed Eddie's trademark splash onto Kelly Kelly for the victory.

VIKTOR

Viktor delivers a modified flying uppercut as part of The Ascension's devastating "Fall of Man" finishing move.

Viktor's ring gear is symbolic of the Egyptian sun god, Ra. Whether Viktor derives his vision from the golden eye of this ancient deity is unknown.

Viktor views the world through a more distinct set of lenses than most people. The twisted and peculiar Superstar sees a society wrought with chaos and disorder. Together with his equally demented partner, Konnor, he plans to shape the universe into his own vision, piece by ruthless piece. If step one was becoming the most dominant tag team in the short history of NXT, then Viktor may be well on his way to fulfilling his prophecy. He and Konnor, better known as The Ascension, ran roughshod over the NXT tag team division for the better part of 2013 and 2014, leaving many to wonder if there is anyone who can stop them but themselves. "Bring your best and watch us mow them down," has been their mantra. They have backed this up in the ring, decimating all comers. The Usos, Wyatts, and other stables of WWE's main roster had better take notice.

HEIGHT: 6 feet, 2 inches (188 cm)

WEIGHT: 219 pounds (99 kg)

HOMETOWN: Calgary, Alberta, Canada

NXT CAREER HIGHLIGHTS: NXT Tag Team Champion

ARRIVED

The Ascension prevailed in their first major title defense at the groundbreaking NXT event, *NXT Arrival.* They continued to annihilate opponents throughout the year, also dominating at the first *NXT Takeover* against Kalisto and El Local.

VISCERA

Viscera used white contact lenses and freaked people out with his icy stare.

Viscera shaved his head into a platinum Mohawk.

Viscera's signature black is a stark contrast to his M.O.M. gear, which looked like purple pajamas.

He was known by several names, but the intimidation he instilled never changed. Viscera began his career in the early 1990s as Mabel, one half of the rapping duo Men on a Mission. During the Attitude Era, this mean mastodon became one of Undertaker's most faithful followers. Reborn as Viscera, he did the Deadman's bidding as part of the sinister stable, The Ministry of Darkness. Brainwashed into the dark side, Viscera's colossal size and gothic appearance evoked fear and awe from the Ministry's victims. The imposing Superstar had a change of heart in 2006, discovering his romantic side and wooing Lilian Garcia. In 2007, Viscera once again reinvented himself. As Big Daddy V, he displayed his expansive, tattooed torso and let his size do the talking. He found an ally in Mark Henry and had memorable run-ins with the man who was first responsible for unleashing his evil side, Undertaker.

HEIGHT:
6 feet, 9 inches (206 cm)

WEIGHT: 487 pounds (221 kg)

HOMETOWN: Harlem, NY

KING SIZED

As Mabel, this mountainous Superstar was the heftiest King of the Ring of all time. His unfortunate subjects, tasked with carrying him to the ring on their shoulders, always appeared close to collapsing under the bulk. Before Matt and Jeff Hardy broke into WWE as competitors, they took on the arduous task of transporting King Mabel.

WESLEY BLAKE

Wesley Blake is a southern-bred NXT Superstar who is savoring his every moment in his fledgling sports-entertainment career. Blake is a relative newcomer to the WWE Performance Center. By day, he soaks in his every chance to train hard and to learn from the best trainers in the business. At night, he gets his chance to "Cowboy Up" and impress the rabid NXT fans in Orlando, Florida. He does it all with a smile etched on his face. Wesley Blake combines a blue-collar work ethic with a go-getter's enthusiasm. This recipe has made him a tough competitor for any NXT Superstar standing within the yellow NXT ring ropes. Blake has found success in fits and starts, as well as a few setbacks. He anticipates many ups and downs in the journey ahead, and is eager to tackle each challenge with the same amped-up energy.

Wesley Blake rode into NXT with his "Cowboy Up" motto serving as inspiration. Blake is a true Texan and has all the right headwear to fit that motto.

HEIGHT: 6 feet, 1 inch (185 cm)
WEIGHT: 240 pounds (109 kg)
HOMETOWN: San Antonio, TX

TAG TEAM BREAKTHROUGH

Wesley Blake got off to a rough start when first facing active competition. He finally got his hand raised for the first time when teaming with Camacho in a tag team match against Baron Corbin and Sawyer Fulton. Knowing what victory feels like motivates him to work even harder toward his goal.

WILLIAM REGAL

William Regal might seem like a refined, tea sipping English gentleman, but underneath the surface lives one of the nastiest competitors in history. A product of the fierce, coastline town of Blackpool, Regal hardened his fighting spirit as part of a traveling carnival act. He took on the deadliest grapplers from Britain's toughest streets, and if that was not enough, challenged complete strangers from the audience! Regal had no choice but to perfect a lethal arsenal of excruciating submission holds. These skills came in handy when he crossed the pond to join WWE, as did his infamous brass knuckles. In 2008, he lived up to his kingly surname by winning the *King of the Ring* tournament. He has also presided over WWE's roster as both *Raw* General Manager and WWE Commissioner. Regal imparts his knowledge on WWE's future stars, and the NXT rookies know not to get on his bad side.

William Regal packs a powerful punch, with or without his notorious knucks.

HEIGHT:
6 feet, 3 inches
(191 cm)

WEIGHT: 243 pounds
(110 kg)

HOMETOWN:
Blackpool, England

SIGNATURE MOVES:
Regal Stretch

POSITIONS HELD:
WWE Commissioner,
Raw General Manager

William Regal wears stately attire as if sitting beside Her Majesty, the Queen.

ATTITUDE INDIGNITIES

Being a man of nobility did not make William Regal immune to some Attitude Era buffoonery. He was duped into drinking tainted tea with a very unpleasant additive, courtesy of Chris Jericho. He also suffered the embarrassment of coming face to face with Mr. McMahon's backside. The classy Brit got a measure of revenge on Y2J in a Duchess of Queensbury Match.

X-PAC

X-Pac showed his attitude by wrapping a do-rag around his rock star hair.

When Triple H needed an X factor to make D-Generation X complete, he turned to The Kliq. X-Pac was revealed as the fifth member of the revamped pack of renegades the night after *WrestleMania XIV*. The Game enlisted him along with the New Age Outlaws to fill a void in the group. X-Pac wasted no time showing his black and lime green loyalty. He earned his colors by shredding his ex-employers at WCW with some pointed remarks. X-Pac was as unfiltered and unapologetic as any of his intrepid comrades. He also brought a different dynamic to the ring, flying around with reckless abandon. His ability to thrive above the mat furthered the rebels' cause. With X-Pac in the fold, even high flyers were no longer safe from a count of 1-2-3 and a two-word salute. He's been known by several names, but it was X-Pac that put the X in DX.

X-Pac proudly displayed the classic DX logo on his gear during his time with the group.

HEIGHT: 6 feet, 1 inch (185 cm)

WEIGHT: 212 pounds (96 kg)

HOMETOWN: Minneapolis, MN

SIGNATURE MOVE: Bronco Buster

UNHOLY ALLIANCE

X-Pac befriended the demonic Kane in 1999, and even struck tag team gold with the Big Red Monster. Despite this success, and the strides X-Pac made with Kane's speaking ability, he still betrayed his newfound ally and stole Kane's girlfriend in the process.

XAVIER WOODS

Xavier Woods highlights his flashy style with one of the most impressive afros in WWE history.

Xavier Woods is a double threat Superstar with a dynamic combination of exciting athleticism and impressive smarts. Woods is the ultimate student-athlete. He owns multiple academic degrees, including a bachelor's in philosophy and psychology, as well as a master's and Ph.D. in educational psychology. With a background in "Hip Hop Kido," he brings a well-rounded skill set to the ring. Despite his flair for the classroom, do not mistake this competitor for a stick in the mud. Xavier knows how to party as well. He lets the good times roll each time he competes, showcasing his up-tempo style for the WWE Universe. WWE veteran R-Truth took a liking to the hungry young star. He and Woods have formed a bond, and Woods has benefited from his coaching at ringside. How much fun lays ahead for Xavier remains to be seen. For now, "It's Morphin' time!"

Xavier's look is inspired by his passion for '90s cartoons and video games, such as *Sonic the Hedgehog* and *Dragonball-Z.*

HEIGHT: 5 feet, 11 inches (180 cm)

WEIGHT: 205 pounds (93 kg)

HOMETOWN: Angel Grove, CA

SIGNATURE MOVE: Honor Roll, Lost in the Woods

TOO FUNKY

Woods's brief alliance with Tons of Funk quickly turned sour. Brodus Clay lashed out in a jealous rage over Woods using his entrance music. The Funkasaurus brutalized the newcomer but Woods got the last laugh. He scored a revenge victory and soon after, Brodus took a hiatus from WWE.

YOKOZUNA

Yokozuna was named for the highest rank in Japanese sumo wrestling. The massive Superstar tipped the scales at close to 600 pounds, by far the heftiest WWE Champion of all time. Sumo wrestlers are known for their incredible size, and Yokozuna had plenty of it. What made him even more terrifying, though, was his agility. Despite his gargantuan frame, he was capable of pinpointing a swift, rising sidekick to a moving target, no small feat for a big man. Yokozuna bulldozed the competition right from his debut in 1992. To the delight of his devious manager, Mr. Fuji, his devastating Banzai Drop pancaked opponents in the middle of the ring. Yokozuna was so dominant it took two matches in one *WrestleMania* to keep him from walking out the WWE Champion two years in a row. America was not safe from his rampage, however. He flattened Hulk Hogan and terrorized as champ for several months.

The "tsuna," worn around the waist, is a symbol of a Yokozuna's prestigious rank.

HEIGHT: 6 feet, 4 inches (193 cm)

WEIGHT: 589 pounds (267 kg)

HOMETOWN:
The Land of the Rising Sun

SIGNATURE MOVE: Banzai Drop

Yokozuna kept his mammoth legs contained in bright red tights.

ROYAL POWER

Yokozuna won his first ever Royal Rumble Match with one of the most impressive eliminations in history. Lying on his back with Randy Savage draped over him, he powered the Macho Man up like a bench press, throwing him in the air and over the ropes.

ZACK RYDER

Spiked WWWYKI wigs were all the rage until Zack Ryder grew out his hair for a more down to earth look.

A true "Broski" pumps his fist with pride for Long Island Iced-Z.

In 2011, Zack Ryder's window of opportunity in WWE seemed to be winding to a close. Knowing his big break would not be left at his doorstep in Long Island, the determined "Broski" decided to show the WWE Universe exactly what they were missing. He used the power of YouTube and social media to create his own platform. His show "Z! True Long Island Story" became an instant sensation. "Likes" and hashtags soon translated to chants and signs. Zack Ryder became the embodiment of a 21st century Superstar, creating his own demand through technology. His self-made success compelled him to create a self-made "Internet Championship," but he soon snagged one of history's most prominent titles. With chants of "Woo! Woo! Woo!" reigning down on him, Zack defeated Dolph Ziggler for the United States Championship. Zack Ryder's unlikely story might make you ask, "Are you serious, bro?" But it's true. You know it!

HEIGHT: 6 feet, 2 inches (188 cm)
WEIGHT: 214 pounds (97 kg)
HOMETOWN: Long Island, NY
SIGNATURE MOVE: Rough Ryder

EDGEHEADS

Zack Ryder and Curt Hawkins eerily resembled Edge early in their careers. Always an opportunist, Edge used the dual doppelgangers to help protect his World Heavyweight Championship. Proving they were not just Rated-R flunkies, the Long Island natives enjoyed a reign as Tag Team Champions.

ZEB COLTER

Zeb's mustache reminds fans of a classic cartoon cowboy and his ill-fated attempts to gun down a pesky rabbit.

Zeb's brainwashed followers chant "We the people" with a hand over their hearts.

Zeb Colter leads his charges into battle wearing a militant khaki vest.

America is a land of opportunity, and Zeb Colter would like to offer you the opportunity to leave. That is, if you do not subscribe to his radical vision of a "Real American." We, the people, come from all walks of life, and some do not quite fit into Colter's right wing agenda. With Jack Swagger's muscle looming behind him, the extremist is not afraid to direct his fanatical rants toward anyone within earshot. Most beg to differ with his drastic beliefs, but not Swagger. Zeb's teachings helped him revitalize his career in 2012. Later on, the Swiss-born Cesaro bought into the cause as well. He may resemble the disgruntled neighborhood loony screaming at those kids to get off his lawn, but Zeb Colter is a war veteran and an experienced competitor. His ideals, while extreme, are rooted in deep passion. America is also a land of free speech, and Zeb takes full advantage.

HEIGHT: 6 feet (183 cm)

WEIGHT: 220 pounds (100 kg)

HOMETOWN: Nashville, TN

SUPERSTARS MANAGED: Jack Swagger, Cesaro

DISSENTION IN THE RANKS

The cracks in Colter's Real Americans team began to show long before the partnership severed. The crusty ring vet showed savvy coaching skills to keep Swagger and Cesaro from tearing each other apart. His effort was commendable, but he was unable to stop Paul Heyman from signing away his prized recruit, Cesaro.

WWE ULTIMATE SUPERSTAR GUIDE

WRITTEN BY STEVE PANTALEO
ILLUSTRATED BY DAZ TIBBLES

BOOKS

Development Editor
Jennifer Sims

Senior Graphic Designer
Carol Stamile

Production Designer
Julie Clark

**Vice President
and Publisher**
Mike Degler

Licensing Manager
Christian Sumner

Digital Publishing Manager
Tim Cox

Marketing Manager
Katie Hemlock

Operations Manager
Stacey Beheler

Global Publishing Manager
Steve Pantaleo

**Senior Director,
Domestic Licensing**
Jess Richardson

**Senior Vice President,
Global Licensing**
Howard Brathwaite

**Executive Vice President,
Consumer Products**
Casey Collins

Photography
Josh Tottenham
Jamie Nelson
JD Sestito
Mike Moran

**Senior Vice President,
Creative Services**
Stan Stanski

**Creative Director,
Global Licesing**
Joe Giorno

**Vice President,
Intellectual Property**
Lauren Dienes-Middlen

DK/BradyGames, a division of Penguin Group (USA).
800 East 96th Street, 3rd Floor
Indianapolis, IN 46240

ISBN: 978-1-4654-3124-0

Printing Code: The rightmost double-digit number is the year of the book's printing; the rightmost single-digit number is the number of the book's printing. For example, 15-1 shows that the first printing of the book occurred in 2015.

18 17 16 15   4 3 2 1

Printed in China.

BradyGames would like to thank Steve Pantaleo, Josh Tottenham, and the rest of the amazing WWE team for all their help and support during this project.

London, New York, Melbourne, and Delhi

Penguin
Random
House

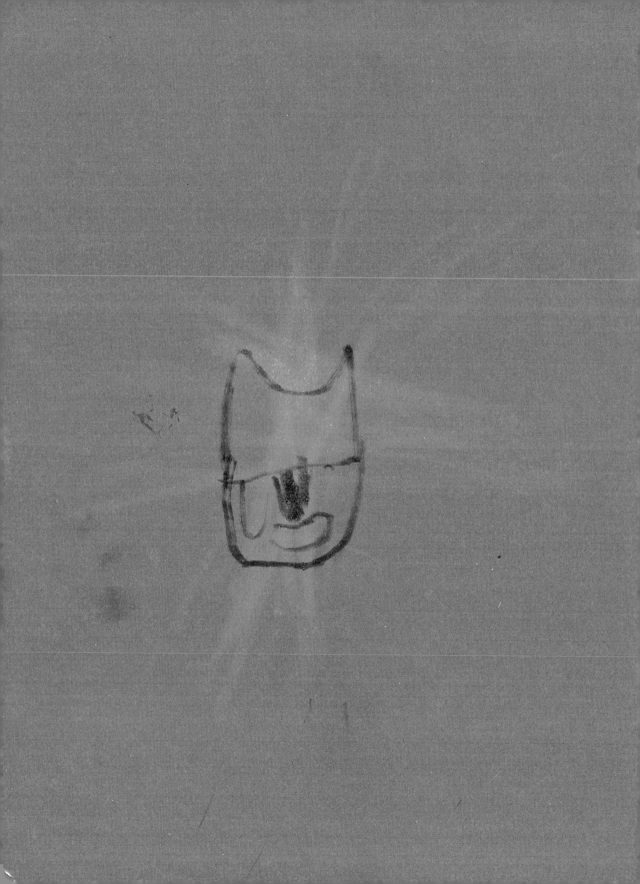